THE GOSPEL

ACCORDING TO

COCO CHANEL

THE GOSPEL

ACCORDING TO

COCO CHANEL

LIFE LESSONS FROM THE WORLD'S MOST ELEGANT WOMAN

KAREN KARBO
ILLUSTRATED BY CHESLEY McLAREN

GUILFORD, CONNECTICUT
An imprint of The Globe Pequot Press

skirt!® is an attitude . . . spirited, independent, outspoken, serious,
playful and irreverent, sometimes controversial, always passionate.

To buy books in quantity for corporate use
or incentives, call **(800) 962-0973**
or e-mail **premiums@GlobePequot.com.**

Text design by Sheryl P. Kober

Library of Congress Cataloging-in-Publication Data is available on file.
ISBN 978-1-59921-523-5

Printed in the United States of America
10 9

For Danna
Where she sits, it is chic
and
To the memory of my grandmother,
Emilia Burzanski Karbowski, also known as Luna of California

Gabrielle Chanel, known as Coco (1883–1971), top French couturier, at Fauborg, St Honore, Paris. PHOTO BY SASHA/GETTY IMAGES

CONTENTS

1. On Style 1

2. On Self-Invention 25

3. On Fearlessness 43

4. On Surviving Passion 61

5. On Embracing the Moment 79

6. On Success 93

7. On Cultivating Arch Rivals 111

8. On Money 133

9. On Femininity 155

10. On Time 175

11. On Living Life on Your Own Terms 193

12. On Elegance: The Gospel According
    to Coco Chanel 221

Acknowledgments 227

About the Author 231

1

ON STYLE

"A girl should be two things: classy and fabulous."

There is an early picture of Gabrielle Chanel taken in a park in Vichy, France. Gabrielle is twenty-three, standing beside her favorite aunt, Adrienne, only a few years older. I'm thrilled to report that the woman Giorgio Armani called "the most elegant woman who's ever lived" was not a classic beauty. She-who-was-not-yet-known-as-Coco had a thicket of dark hair, black eyes, and a wide pirate mouth. She looked like the girl at school who conned you into breaking the rules with her, then let you take all the blame. Both the writer Colette and Diana Vreeland (editor of *Harper's Bazaar* and *Vogue*) thought she looked like a bull. Perhaps back then bulls, like closets and serving sizes, were much smaller; Chanel was scampish, lithe, and agile. Vreeland, remembering Chanel at fifty would say, "She was bright, dark gold-color—wide face, with a snorting nose, just like a little bull, and deep Dubonnet-red cheeks."

But in this picture, Coco is clearly not the Pretty One. The two young women occupy the left side of the frame. A man with poor posture, wearing a bowler, crosses the path behind them.

The picture titillates. You can already see the early stirrings of the iconic Chanel style. The more classically beautiful Adrienne is swimming in the typical park-strolling attire of the time—a double-breasted tunic layered over a full, floor-length skirt, bloused up over a belt obscured by a bunch of extra fabric, some kind of a high-collared shirt tightly buttoned around her neck, and one of those infamous fin de siècle hats that looked like a platter of pastries. Her clothes seem to have no particular relationship to her body; they express nothing aside from the fashion of the time.

Gabrielle, on the other hand, looks fresh and almost rakish. Her skirt is trim, A-line, and ankle length. Her matching jacket is hip length with a notched collar, nipped in slightly at the waist. Her blouse is plain, her belt wide; her hat is a straw boater pinned up on one side, like a Musketeer. She's wearing something frilly around her neck that feminizes the whole streamlined ensemble. Her outfit seems well considered, the proportions just right.

You can't help thinking that Chanel's taste must have been genetic, that she discovered as a young woman what became her and never lost faith in it the way some of us do. She never woke up one morning, sick of her impossibly well-cut jackets and pearls and thought, "What I really need is a hat in the shape of a shoe or a flame-colored rayon sari trimmed with tiny gold cymbals." The times surged and changed beneath her, but over the decades Chanel merely elaborated upon what she preferred, what she knew to look good on her, and what she found to be both comfortable and practical. If nothing else, the woman was a complete stranger to the embarrassing impulse buy, and for that alone we should salute her.

It's impossible to resist further overanalyzing the picture: In it Adrienne is gazing at Gabrielle, while Gabrielle is looking straight at the photographer and thus out at the world.

✹✹✹

For nearly a hundred years, Coco Chanel has been synonymous with every piece of clothing we consider stylish—and with lots of stuff to which we never give a thought. Throw open your closet door and you will find the spirit of Chanel. If you have a collection of jackets for tossing on over a pair of jeans, the better to look as if you've actually dressed for the occasion—as opposed to simply parked the lawn mower, given your nails a once over with the nail brush, and walked out the door—that's Chanel. Any black dress is a direct descendent of Chanel's 1926 short silk model. A knee-grazing pencil or A-line skirt? Chanel. Jersey anything? Chanel again.

She gave us real pockets, bell-bottoms, twin sets, drop waists, belted cardigans, short dresses for evening, sportswear including riding breeches, and the need to accessorize madly at all times. Anything that's got simple lines, skims the body, is easy to move in, and affords the loading on of a lot of jewelry is Chanel.

So too is anything in which prettiness trumps quirkiness. Chanel ran screaming from the latest fads. She considered them to be expressions of cheesy grandstanding, and, anyway, they rarely held to her standards of simple elegance. Thus ponchos, stirrup pants, or backless dresses cut in a manner that reveals your thong are definitely not

Chanel. If you own anything that has epaulets (and you are not in the armed forces), an unnecessary amount of fabric, ill-fitting arms, or Hulk-size shoulder pads, it is not Chanel. Anything related to the grunge revival, featuring ripped tights that look as if you've barely survived a mugging? Uh, no.

Anything in which you cannot breathe, sit down, or get into a car without flashing your lady bits—well, I don't even need to say it. When Chanel observed that "not all women have the figure of Venus* yet nothing should be hidden," this is *not* what she was talking about. (To clarify, she meant that the loose, long T-shirts we reserve for fat days do nothing but make us look fatter.)

The Chanel aesthetic is like the force in *Star Wars,* surrounding, penetrating, and binding together the universe of fashion, now and forever. As I write this I'm wearing a pair of J. Crew boy jeans—even though they're square through the hip with straight legs and a button fly, they are cunningly cut to prevent your looking like an appliance box—and a chocolate brown, long-sleeve cashmere T-shirt. Both pieces descend straight from Chanel's once-shocking ideas that with a smidge of fancying up, menswear could be easily retooled for the ladies and soft, body-defining fabrics (some of which were normally used for underwear) could make the simplest garment seem *luxe.*

When we enter the realm of garments issued from the House of Chanel itself, things get more complicated. I think of everything that was designed by Coco herself, from her first straw boater in the early 1900s

---

Actually, a lot of us do; what we don't have is the flat-chested, slim-hipped figure of Chanel.

to the last jacket of her last collection in 1970, to be Chanel-Chanel. All pieces that date from 1983, when the redoubtable Karl Lagerfeld took over and revitalized the fashion house, are Lagerfeld-Chanel.* There are, in addition, high-end knockoffs that pass as Chanel-Chanel (discussion still rages over whether the pink Chanel suit Jackie Kennedy wore on the day her husband was shot was a genuine Chanel or a copy whipped up by a New York dressmaker) and knockoffs of Lagerfeld's semiannual collections, which usually riff on Mademoiselle's lady-like suits, gold chains, quilted bags, and the iconic interlocking Cs. There are also—stay with me—mass-market copies of the higher end knockoffs. Mavens of haute couture and certain bloggers spend a shocking number of hours keeping it all straight.

Here is my stab at sorting it all out.

Chanel Classic

This is Chanel in its pure, undiluted early-to-mid-twentieth-century form. It is not only fashion the way Coco intended, it consists only of garments made with Chanel's own nicotine-stained fingers. (She was a mad chain-smoker. I defy you to find a picture of her working without a ciggie clamped between her teeth.)

---

* *Between 1971 and 1983 the House wandered in the wilderness, so to speak. Gaston Berthelot designed from 1971–1973; Jean Cazaubon and Yvonne Dudel took over from there; Philippe Guibourgé designed a ready-to-wear in 1978; and someone named Ramone Esparza showed up in 1980.*

Chanel Classic is the iconic Chanel suit made of loosely woven tweed (probably in beige, navy blue, or black—the colors Coco preferred), with its quilted silk lining, gold-chain hem, and simple knee-grazing skirt. It is the big clunky costume jewelry, sporting poured glass that looks like hard candy, and the square quilted bags, so classic that an illustration of one could appear on the international sign for handbags. It is the aforementioned black dress in crepe de chine or lace. Hats always figure into Chanel Classic style, including one with a yachting motif that looks as if it would be happy on the head of Thurston Howell III; also, two-tone beige and black pumps, with a comfortable, modest heel that is about as far away from a pair of *Sex in the City*-sanctioned *do me* Manolo Blahniks as a black Rolls is from a stoplight yellow Corvette. It is the long ropes of pearls, which always look as if they pose a risk of strangulation, and of course, the camellias.

Chanel Classic is collectible Chanel (and thus the posh-city cousin of Fiesta ware, Wagon Wheel furniture, and comic books). It's investment Chanel. It's sell-it-on-eBay-in-order-to-pay-the-kid's-college-tuition Chanel. People own private Chanel Classic collections in the same way they own private art collections. It is less about the clothes than it is about the iconic design; *iconic* being the most overused word in the Chanel canon.

Not many women have the proper combination of time, devotion, money, and obsessive-compulsive disorder to dress every day in head-to-toe Chanel Classic, but at least those who do always look chic, if a tad nutty. In a recent *New York Times* review of the Lifetime

Channel movie about Coco, starring Shirley MacLaine, the reviewer said, "She was never a wife, but she made the women of the world look like one."

Chanel Homage

According to Dana Thomas, in *Deluxe: How Luxury Lost Its Luster*, only two hundred women in the world maintain wardrobes of haute couture (this down from two hundred thousand in the 1950s). Every other well-dressed woman of means buys high-end prêt-à-porter, ready-to-wear, which can still set you back an easy six figures a year.

Chanel, today, is Brand Chanel. It's Karl Lagerfeld expanding on the prestige and history of Coco's achievements. Busy, busy Lagerfeld. Since becoming the art director for the House of Chanel, he has also established his own label; designed for Fendi, Chloe, and recently H&M; created his own advertising campaigns (which he also photographed); designed costumes for operas; opened a bookstore, then a publishing house; and then lost about a hundred pounds and wrote a best-selling diet book about the experience.

Lagerfeld's Chanel is the Chanel essence pressed through the sieve of his own (admittedly appealing) haut-Eurotrash sensibility. Chanel's practical designs sprang from the changing reality of her own life and the lives of the women around her, and Lagerfeld's spring from the brand that is Chanel, mixed with whatever else is going on out there zeitgeist-wise. Sometimes his designs are practical and sometimes they are not, but each collection is the couturier version of a seventh-grade writing prompt: For spring, please create a hip-hop–inspired collection that incorporates quilting, cardigans, and two-tone shoes.

Thus over the years Lagerfeld-Chanel has shown a bra top accessorized with a lightbulb pendant on a thick gold chain; tighty whities embroidered with a pair of black interlocking Cs worn with black tights (an homage to Chanel's original use of jersey, once considered only fit for underwear); quilted biker clothes, including biker boots decorated with the interlocking gold Cs; and a black dress studded with jeweled chain mail.

It's all a referential hoot, especially the hat fashioned from the black leather quilted bag, complete with gold chain that sort of dangles over one eyebrow, making the wearer look like a resident of Whoville. The metallic perforated lambskin open-toe wedge ankle boot from the Spring-Summer 2008 Ready-to-Wear line, shown with a denim bikini, gave me pause, but beachwear was never Chanel's strong suit, and Lagerfeld is apparently no different.

A lot of Lagerfeld flies in the face of Chanel's nearly religious devotion to simplicity. Is there anyone, anywhere you can think of who needs a quilted ankle purse or a black feathered, face-covering cage hat? (Designed by Chanel's resident hat guy, Philip Treacy, it's part of that mid-1990s bondage thing Lagerfeld had going on.)

Still, the man is no fool. The underpants suit and face-covering cage hat gained him ink, while the variations on the still-pretty tweed suit gained him customers. Next fall's ready-to-wear collection is full of belted, knee-length suits with longer, fitted jackets worn with pale tights and what look like two-tone tap-dancing shoes. I could think of no better way to spend a year's salary.

Alt Chanel

Chanel was first and foremost a realist, and everything having to do with Chanel style is realistic. She was never unaware of what things cost. One of the reasons she began using jersey was that she could get it cheap. In 1916 or thereabouts Chanel bought up the unsold stock of machine-knit jersey from fabric manufacturer Jean Rodier, whipped it up into one of her famous body-skimming frocks, and made it chic. Then she charged a fortune.

In the spirit of Chanel, Alt Chanel embraces the reality that to get yourself done up in Chanel Homage you'd have to be a Hollywood starlet famous for her red-carpet appearances, an Arabian princess, the heiress to a Mexican cell-phone empire, or the wife of a richer-than-average rich man— i.e., someone whose income resides in the top 1 percent of the top 1 percent of the richest people around, i.e., richer than you and me. Alt Chanel is for the stylish among us for whom income isn't disposable.

The key factor in wearing Alt Chanel is cheekiness. There's a good chance that even if you had all the money in the world you'd still prefer the insouciance, the *irony* involved in wearing a vintage Chanel tweed jacket over jeans and a white T-shirt from the Gap or, as a friend did recently, pairing a gypsy skirt and sun-bleached red

Converse high-tops with a black quilted Chanel purse. Alt Chanel style communicates to the world that you're *hip* to Chanel but aren't a *slave* to Chanel. It says, "Chanel was an iconoclast, and I am, too."

It only seems fair, before we get too much further, to point out that even though Chanel gets credit for inventing the wheel of modern fashion, other designers of the time were also out there wrenching women out of hourglass corsets and into clothing that made them look more like a human being and less like the prow of a ship (considered in the Belle Époque to be the height of feminine beauty).

Paul Poiret, nicknamed *Le Magnifique*, made the world safe for Chanel. He paved the way for her revolution. He was her warm-up act, the guy they send out before the headliner to get people in the mood to laugh. In 1903 Poiret, the son of a cloth merchant in Les Halles, opened his own house, where he shocked Parisian society by offering a long coat that resembled a kimono. He invented the over-the-top window display and threw huge, inappropriate parties to draw attention to himself. It was Poiret, and *not* Chanel, who freed women from their corsets (and then perversely reenslaved them in the sugar cone–shaped hobble skirt, full around the hips and so narrow around the ankles that one had to be lifted into carriages).

Poiret designed the first pair of women's trousers, but they were harem pants and required the wearer to dress as a Turk. He designed the lamp shade tunic. (Did any woman, then or now, really want to look like anything aligned in any way with home decor?) His creativity wasn't confined to fashion; he dabbled in the decorative arts, introducing both the wet bar and the sunken bathtub, innovations that Americans still love. In 1910, years before Coco stumbled upon the idea for No. 5, Poiret struck upon the idea of creating his own scent, Coupe d'Or.

Poiret was no fan of Chanel's. Long before Elsa Schiaparelli showed up, he was Coco's main competitor. He accused her of making fashion that was nothing more than deluxe poverty, of transforming all women into nothing more than undernourished-looking telegraph clerks. Before slipping into Chanel's eclipsing shadow, Poiret said of her, "We ought to have been on our guard against that boyish head. It was going to give us every kind of shock, and produce, out of its little conjurer's hat, gowns and coiffures and sweaters and jewels and boutiques."

Setting aside for a moment the fact that Poiret couldn't seem to get out of his own way, Chanel had another indisputable advantage: She was a woman, designing for women, and she wasn't afraid to be her own best model. (Madeleine Vionnet, Chanel's contemporary, routinely credited with inventing the bias cut, was horrified at the idea of such self-promotion.) Chanel wore the clothes she designed for the life she led. She said, "I don't do fashion, I am fashion." Poiret, alas, did fashion. And after Chanel arrived on the scene a lot of his fashion didn't do.

✳✳✳

Coco Chanel got her start in hats. She had a flair for knowing exactly what to do with a single feather or silk flower. Her first establishment was on the Boulevard Malesherbes, in the Paris apartment of her first lover, Étienne Balsan, diffident aristocrat, passionate breeder of thoroughbreds, and flaunter of convention. Balsan's family had made their fortune in textiles. His younger brother, Jacques, married a Vanderbilt (Consuelo, former duchess of Marlborough), but Étienne was a rule breaker. He fancied aging courtesans and black-eyed waifs with nothing to offer but spunk.

Balsan spied Chanel singing at a caf'conc* in Vichy. Or he made her acquaintance at a tea party, where they discussed horses and fate. Or he met her when he brought his trousers in to be tailored at the little shop where she worked to make ends meet. Accounts differ. With Chanel, accounts always differ, in part because she was a master of misinformation, which is a nice way of saying she compulsively lied about her past, and then lied about having lied, and then disavowed the lie about the lie. In her later years she hired and fired a number of writers to write her memoirs, telling each one something different, as the spirit moved her. And she always lied about her age. For the first part of her life, she looked and claimed to be at least ten years younger than she actually was, then, sometime in her fifties, she started telling people she was a hundred. What has grown up in the

---

Short for café concert, literally "singing café," a Belle Époque staple, where small combos performed the pop songs of the day.

place of verifiable facts is Chanelore, a combination of truth, embellishment, lies, and legend.

When Chanel met Balsan she was perhaps twenty-two and was kicking around Vichy—playground of Napoleon III and other nineteenth-century celebrities and known for its thermal waters and landscaped gardens—hoping to become a singer. It was a completely understandable, run-of-the-mill aspiration, the early twentieth-century version of hoping to make it on *American Idol.*

A typical caf'conc featured a comedian, a baritone or two, and a few sexy girl singers who vamped around the small stage, competing with clattering plates, bustling waiters, and the endless interruption of peddlers. Singing at a caf'conc required no special training other than the ability to belt out the popular songs of the day and the force of personality to coax patrons into lingering and spending more money. Becoming a star ensured a good income and perhaps a sitting for Toulouse-Lautrec, where you would pose straddling a chair, your black stockings pooled around your ankles and your hair caught up in a messy topknot.

Even though Chanel had no experience and no evidence of any singing or performing talent whatsoever, she talked her way into auditions at the best caf'concs in town. Her confidence only got her so far. For probably the last time in her long life, she failed to impress. She was cute but lacked the ability to strut her stuff. She sang like a frog battling laryngitis, and she could never manage the required slinking around. She was eventually hired to be a *gommeuse*—a pretty girl who possessed more looks than voice, who would slink around in risqué finery and chirp out a song or two to justify her presence.

Chanel must have already known that her future didn't lie in show biz, so when Balsan asked her to come to Royallieu, his chateau/thoroughbred-breeding operation, she said, *"Pourquoi pas?"* Why not? There, she was installed as Balsan's second-string mistress. His first-string mistress was the world-class courtesan Emilienne d'Alençon, also installed at Royallieu. Before becoming a demimondaine, d'Alençon enjoyed a very short career in the circus where, dressed in a skimpy clown outfit, she performed an act with trained rabbits. A wealthy French duke sent flowers to her dressing room, and it was a short hop from an impoverished existence in an unheated room to an apartment in a fashionable Parisian neighborhood, a wardrobe allowance, and her own horse-drawn carriage. She was beautiful, ambitious, and without scruples. Chanel liked her immensely, but even by French standards, the whole arrangement was pretty weird.

Chanel spent most of her days at the stables with the horse trainers and grooms. She loved Balsan's thoroughbreds, but had no aptitude for the indolent kept-woman lifestyle generally practiced by mistresses of wealthy men. Her main job seemed to be to entertain Balsan's pals with her extreme youth (next to the big 'n blowsy, Mae Westian d'Alençon, Chanel looked like an underfed street urchin), sass, and ability to jump on the back of a barely broke two-year-old stallion and gallop off through the forest.

Balsan set Chanel and her hat business up in his little-used Parisian apartment to humor her. Like most people born into wealth,

Balsan was mystified by his *petite amie*'s desire to *do* something. What he never bothered to figure out was that the woman who would one day say "Fashion is made to become unfashionable" knew full well that after a few years she would go out of fashion with him, as d'Alençon already had, and then where would she be?

Chanel opened the doors to her business in 1909 or 1910, although it could have also been as late as 1912 or as early as 1905 when the *International Herald Tribune* ran a small story reporting that one could purchase a nice fur muff at Chanel Modes. Anyway, it was sometime during the late Belle Époque, when fashionable women spent most of their time obsessively changing their clothes. There was an outfit for breakfast, for promenading in the park, for visiting the dressmaker, for tea, for making or receiving social calls between five o'clock and seven o'clock (also the two hours traditionally set aside for adultery), for dinner, and for the theater. Of course each ensemble required its own hat.

A typical hat of the pre-Chanel era might have been two feet across; made of velvet, felt, mohair, or long-napped beaver; and provided an ample "plateau" for lace, velvet, and silk flowers—roses and hydrangeas were popular—and feathers, feathers, feathers. In 1911 in France alone, three hundred million birds were sacrificed for their wing, plume, and cock feathers.* Buckles of various metals, including steel, were used to fasten a velvet ribbon around the crown. The weight of such hats would tax the neck of even the sturdiest matron, but no one gave it a thought.

---

*A factoid reported in the Paris Herald, *which freaked out the few environmentalists of the day.*

Hats were worn at an angle and hovered over the wearer's head with the aid of something called a Pompadour Hair Frame Support, which allowed the hair beneath the hat to be built up into a small hat-supporting hair tower. Women requested that their maids save hair from their brushes, in case even more hair was needed to create the proper amount of height and volume. Hat pins were needed to affix the whole megillah to the head; naturally they were also large and ornate, often made of cut crystal set with pearls and diamonds or rose quartz.

Hats were both de rigueur and an astounding nuisance. Women needed to travel with their maids because they couldn't construct their scaffolding of hair and pin on their hats by themselves. Everyone accepted these mammoth headdresses as part of a fashionable woman's life, with the exception of avid lovers of the stage, who every so often launched an impassioned campaign to get women to wear smaller hats to the theater. The campaigns were rarely successful; few women dared remove their hats in public for fear of exposing their fake hair and hair support.

Such nonsense couldn't go on indefinitely—if only for the sake of the nation's bird population.

Coco Chanel was opinionated long before anyone cared what she thought. She wondered both to herself and aloud how a woman could think under one of those things. A hat made by Chanel was so basic it was shocking. She bought flat-topped straw boaters[*] in bulk from the Galeries Lafayette department store, which she trimmed

---

[*] *A small-brimmed hat with a flat top, worn most often these days by the members of a barbershop quartet.*

herself with a single plume or silk flower. They sat straight on the head, no Pompadour Hair Frame Supporters necessary. Their simplicity made them eccentric.

Chanel's first customer was none other than Émilienne d'Alençon, who wore a Chanel creation to the races at Longchamp. D'Alençon had recently left Balsan for a jockey. The gossip couldn't be more delicious. And what was that marvelous and strange hat on d'Alençon's head?

Chanel's immediate success in millinery was more than the sum of her hats. Anyone could troop down to the department store, buy a bunch of straw boaters, and tack a blue grosgrain ribbon around the crowns. That no one else did can be filed under *Genius, the Simplicity of*. But the hats were also Chanel's calling cards, advertisements for herself. Word had gotten around that Balsan was involved with the strangest young thing, neither of good breeding nor traditional sexed-up courtesan appeal. The women attached to the men in Balsan's crowd showed up at Chanel Modes to check out his *petite amie*. Chanel was a curiosity, a unicorn in their midst, and she was more than happy to parlay her then-idiosyncratic look into customers. Ladies came to stare and left with a hat or two. Long before No. 5, something new was in the air.

This is all well and good, but what's it got to do with us? The closest most of us will come to the newest collection from the House of

Chanel is reading *Vogue* on an airplane. I'm exaggerating, but only a little.

The last time I was in New York, I popped into the Chanel Soho Boutique on Spring Street. I toyed with dipping into my money market account for a plum-colored cardigan, but feared being faced with the same dilemma I encounter when painting the living room: Afterward the walls look so great they make all the furniture (even books) look shabby and depressing by comparison. I returned to the shop four times. I floated my living room–painting metaphor past the good-natured salesman. He chuckled professionally and tried to sell me a bottle of Cristalle. I skipped the perfume, and the cardigan, and now I'm kicking myself.

But even if you aren't the type to neurotically overanalyze the purchase of a Chanel sweater, there's still the possibility (admittedly slim) that neither Chanel-Chanel nor Lagerfeld-Chanel suits you. Because Chanel has become synonymous with style and elegance we tend to forget that she designed clothes first and foremost for her own frame. She was tiny, flat of chest, and small of hip. We don't know much about her waist, but it's safe to assume that she was built like a gymnast. Well into her eighties Chanel was fond of saying, "I could still wear the clothes I wore as young girl. Cut off my head, and I'm thirteen years old."

If you are not built like a gymnast, if you are not tiny but instead of average height with broad shoulders and hips and a small waist, or average-size shoulders and hips and a big waist, a Chanel suit might make you feel like a rectangle on legs. Chanel's classic neutral palette of navy blue, gray, and beige may make you look malarial and not chic. Perhaps the mere *thought* of wearing costume jewelry makes you feel as if you're channeling the spirit of Aunt Daphne, the one with the orange lipstick bleeding into the corners of her lips, drunk on highballs, who used to cha-cha around the living room. Chanel might make you feel like a cat lady, when you are emphatically a dog person.

No matter. It's an irony Chanel herself might have appreciated: To embody the Chanel style, it is not necessarily necessary to wear Chanel.

Style à la Chanel

"It's always better to be slightly underdressed."
Overdressing is the first cousin of trying too hard. It is to advertise to the world that you don't trust yourself or your clothes to rise to the occasion. It is to believe that you really can gild a lily, that beauty comes from without and not from within, and that more is better. (Even today the modernist dictate that less is more still holds true, except when it comes to reruns of *The Sopranos*.)

Not to sound too much like an English teacher, but notice Chanel's admonition calls for being *slightly* underdressed. This means jeans worn to a black-tie dinner are neither classy nor fabulous, and even if the bridesmaids at your favorite niece's wedding are all wearing flip-flops, that doesn't give you license to do the same.

"All you have to do is subtract."

Chanel was not just a brilliant designer and tastemaker but also a girl who reveled in the sweeping proclamation, the maxim that sums it all up. Years before Dorothy Parker was cracking wise from her post at the Algonquin Round Table, Chanel was opining in Paris. As a result she is credited with a lot of sayings that may not belong to her. She may or may not have said, "Before you leave the house, look in the mirror and remove one accessory," but the point is certainly Chanelian.

Simplicity will now and forevermore be equated with elegance. Think: Do you really need that chain belt? The tri-layered tank tops? Everything from the bottom tier of your jewelry box (where all the necklaces and bracelets doze in a snake-like tangle) slung around your neck? The patterned purple stockings beneath the thigh-high fringed boots? (Maybe you do; see below.)

"One shouldn't spend all one's time dressing. All one needs are two or three suits, as long as they and everything to go with them, are perfect."

Few things about Chanel style have not withstood the test of time. One is the straw boater (she even wore it at home; that way if someone uninteresting dropped by, she could always say she was going out), and the other is the idea that the foundation of the stylish woman's wardrobe is two or three well-made suits. The concept is just too matchy-matchy for us moderns (thus Alt Chanel).

Still, the point is well-taken. Despite our national obsession with how one looks, spending too much time dressing signals to the world, not to mention friends and family, that you are a self-absorbed twit, plus not very interesting. There are few things less stylish than a boring, self-absorbed twit, and so the idea of assembling a few perfect go-to outfits, the pieces of which can be brought in off the bench, is both elegant and chic. We're talking mix and match. We're saying that every beautiful piece you own should go with every other beautiful piece. Because you have better things to do than think endlessly about your clothes. Right?

"One ought to be a bit of a fetishist."

People who don't like Chanel (yes, they are out there) object to two things. The first is that she is often viewed as being the Mother of Fleece—that her comfy jersey suits paved the way for the American impulse to go to the supermarket in sweatpants and bedroom slippers. Her detractors insist she's responsible for every unstylish slobbola look in contemporary culture, for making the world safe for couples to tour the world in shorts, matching T-shirts, baseball caps, and running shoes. The second objection is that her clothes are not, in fact, simple and elegant, but pedestrian and dull.

Enter the camellia, Chanel's favorite flower and symbol of her elegant, mysterious brand of tomboyish femininity. Proust shocked the Salon des Guermantes by wearing a camellia in his buttonhole (the wearing of a camellia was associated with the sort of extramarital naughtiness for which the French upper classes are famous), rather than the usual staid carnation, and Chanel pounced. She adored the flower's near-perfect roundness, the creamy whiteness against a black dress or dark hair. She pinned one to hat brims, pockets, waistlines, and lapels. She embroidered them on blouses (as early as 1922) and on the toes of shoes. They showed up embossed in gold buttons and dangling in pendants. She commissioned textile makers to design camellia-patterned fabrics and individual artificial camellias in silk, velvet, tulle, chiffon, and leather.

Being a bit of a fetishist allows us to indulge the much bally-hooed individuality without which we Americans would shrivel up and die. Our fetishes give us permission to own a vast collection of red shoes, or Eiffel Tower jewelry.

"Style is knowing who you are, what you want to say, and not giving a damn."

Uttered not by Chanel, but her compatriot in upsetting the apple cart, Gore Vidal. This is the crux of the matter. One of the reasons we hold the magnificently imperfect Chanel up as the perfect manifestation of style is that she was never in doubt about what she liked and what suited her. Even when she was nothing more than Balsan's latest diversion, she appeared on his arm at the races with her small hat jammed on her head, her dark tailor-made suit, and a white blouse. People stared. Where was her platter hat? Her flounces, her tiered silken train, her petticoat, her boa?

To know who we are is a challenge for most of us. As dutiful consumers of media we are dogged by the feeling that we should exist in a state of eternal self-transformation. To plant our flag in the ground—right here, right now—and say "This is me!" seems to us to be settling for less, or giving up, or not being all that we can be.

An effortlessly chic friend had this tip about how to get a handle on your own style: The next time you go away somewhere where you need to look great, underpack. You will have no room to spare for that bubble skirt you like to wear if you're feeling skinny and playful and in a good mood with, you know, just a smidge of tan. You will only be able to take what works, what you feel comfortable and confident in, what makes you feel like you. When you get home, get rid of everything in your closet that doesn't conform to those standards, remembering Chanel's admonition that "nothing makes a woman look older than obvious expensiveness and complication." Also, take care when wearing white, lest you look as if you've been dipped in whipped cream.

2

ON SELF-INVENTION

"How many cares one loses when one decides not to be something but to be someone."

My impulse is to let the above quote sit there like one of Chanel's perfect 2.55 quilted pocketbooks, in the hopes that you'll just admire it without asking too many questions. The bag, introduced to the world in February 1955 (thus 2.55), costs a fortune and cannot be counted on to carry more than your wallet, keys, and lipstick. Even Chanel, as prescient as she was, could not have imagined the day would come when women would also need purse space for a telephone.

This is just the kind of blithe, counterintuitive thing Chanel loved to say, no doubt fully aware that easier said than done doesn't begin to cover it. But what does she really mean? What cares, exactly, did she lose when she decided not to pursue her caf'conc musical career or, more important, the role of a respectable convent-bred girl of modest means hoping to marry up, to a shopkeeper or perhaps even a railroad stationmaster? Obvious ones come to mind: She would no longer have to worry about:

a. The fact that she couldn't really sing.

b. The fact that she wasn't much of a performer at all.

c. The boredom that goes with being viewed as proper, demure, virginal, and thus marriageable.

d. Being nice.

I wish I could write off this last care as a concern of the last century, if not the nineteenth century. Chanel is eternal—yes, iconic—and so we tend to forget that she was born in 1883, under the tyrannical reign of the "Angel in the House." The perfect woman was a perfect wife, first described in a silly poem by Coventry Patmore in 1854, revised in 1862, later immortalized in an essay by Virginia Woolf in 1931 ("She was intensely sympathetic. She was immensely charming. She was utterly unselfish. She excelled in the difficult arts of family life. She sacrificed daily. If there was a chicken, she took the leg; if there was a draught she sat in it. . . . Above all, she was pure."), and more recently riffed upon by writer and editor Cathi Hanauer in her anthology *The Bitch in the House,* a compilation of essays by women who still struggle with the same old question about how nice you actually have to be to remain happily married. I'm simplifying, but that's the gist of it.

I realize I'm trotting out an old dilemma, one that we presumed was solved around the time pantyhose was invented. But this question of being nice, and caring that we are perceived as being nice, is the elephant in the angel's living room. For the past several years I've written a monthly advice column for *Redbook* magazine. I answer four questions a month, on a variety of problems related to relationships, work, and money. The questions have one thing in common: How can the question-asker tell her husband, best friend, sister, mother-in-law, or boss that she's going to do something or not do something, or that they need to do something or stop doing something, without appearing to be a bitch? Some of these problems are huge and intractable. My answer-seekers shoulder enormous burdens, they are married to lovable losers, they're working two jobs, they're getting their degrees at night, and they have children, health problems, debt. They really are struggling, and most of the time the change they want to effect in their lives is completely reasonable. And yet, they wonder how they can solve their problem without making anyone angry. They care about being nice.

Chanel did not care about being nice, or playing by any rules other than the ones she set for herself. The temptation is great to write her chutzpah off to some special circumstance, to her "genius" (unlike Picasso, who could draw a perfect circle in utero, Chanel's gifts were not readily apparent) or some advantage she had, but Chanel had nothing. She had just about every strike against her you could possibly imagine. Her childhood was the Belle Époque version of a country western song. The only thing she lacked was a dead dog and a wasting disease.

Born in the poorhouse hospice in Saumur, an unremarkable town in central France, her parents, Jeanne DeVolle and Henri-Albert Chanel, were unmarried—a fact that could destroy your life in those days. She was named Gabrielle Bonheur, after the nun who delivered her, as her beleaguered mother apparently had no other ideas, and her last name was misspelled Chasnel on her birth certificate. Given the eventual heft of the name Chanel, the irony of this sloppy mistake is delicious, even today.

Albert Chanel, as he was known, was a charismatic schemer who'd also been born in a poorhouse, an itinerant peddler specializing in the sale of buttons, bonnets, aprons, and whatever else he could get his hands on. He mostly worked the market towns of the Auvergne, in the mountainous region of south-central France, famous for its extinct volcanoes, salted hams, and cagey peasants, getting distracted along the way by the usual temptations. Jeanne DeVolle was one of those temptations, the daughter of an innkeeper who rented him a room. Jeanne was nineteen when she gave birth to Gabrielle (she and Albert already had another daughter, Julie, born a year earlier). Albert eventually got around to marrying her, fifteen months after Gabrielle was born, but it did nothing to remove the stain of illegitimacy.

Albert installed Jeanne and her babies in a one-room flat in Issoire, before setting off for Moulins, Brioude, and Aurillac, returning home every so often to impregnate her. In 1885 Jeanne gave birth to Alphonse. In 1887 Jeanne gave birth to Antoinette. In 1889, in a popular tavern, Jeanne gave birth to Lucien. Not long afterward, suffering from what was probably tuberculosis and the stress of being endlessly pregnant and malnourished, Jeanne quietly perished in yet another freezing room where she'd been parked by the peripatetic Albert. She was either twenty-six or thirty-two when she died. In some accounts Gabrielle was six years old, in others she was eleven or twelve. In any case, after Jeanne's death Albert dropped his five kids off at his mom's place in Vichy, never to be seen or heard from again.

Albert's mother, who had a passel of children of her own, couldn't afford to keep her grandchildren; Lucien and Alphonse were sent to a state work farm, while Gabrielle and her sisters, Antoinette and Julie, were shipped off to an orphanage run by the sisters of the Congregation of the Sacred Heart of Mary at Aubazine, in Corrèze.

Even among the orphans, Gabrielle and her sisters were pariahs. Most of the girls at Aubazine possessed extended family who could pay the nuns something for their keep. The Chanels were among the indigent who had no families, or families too poor to contribute anything, who ate watered-down porridge at separate tables and slept in unheated dormitories. Coco and her sisters were the lowest of the low.

Chanel's first conscious act of rebellion was to lie. She lied about or embellished pretty much everything in her childhood, rearranging events, inventing anecdotes and characters, editing out siblings. She had no respect for anything she didn't create, and that included her own history. She became an expert at spreading misinformation about where she came from and who her people were, and for a long time she had the whole world hoodwinked. Even Janet Flanner, writing in the *New Yorker* in 1931, hedged her bet, describing Chanel's girlhood vaguely as "obscure, healthy, bucolic." At the risk of ruining her lovely sentence, Flanner could have stopped at obscure.

Chanel was on the forefront of what we now know as spin. Her inventions were no worse than those of your average politician. She came from nowhere, owned nothing, and had no one. To whom did she owe the truth about her modest beginnings? The aristocrats and society ladies who snubbed her because she was "in trade"? Her artist friends—Cocteau, Picasso, Diaghilev, Stravinsky—who weren't above refashioning their own résumés and preached that art was the lie that told the truth?

Yet the more legendary Chanel became, the more the world disapproved of her stubborn refusal to come clean on the matter of her girlhood misery. No one cared where she was from when she'd been a shopgirl, a seamstress, a caf'conc singer, and the *petite amie* of a rich man. Then she became Chanel, and people started to wonder about her, and the wonder turned into the need to know, and the need to know turned into the right to know. It was the same old thing: The more famous she became, the more the people who made her famous felt she owed them an explanation. It was not very nice of her, was it, not to admit the truth?

Given how her life had turned out, why was she holding out on us? We were bowled over by her fashions, bought No. 5 by the gallon, worshipped her style, emulated her chic, and even embraced her comeback after she'd been disgraced during World War II for taking up with a Nazi. (She was outraged that anyone would take issue with whom she chose as a lover: "When you're my age you don't ask to see a gentleman's passport," she cried.) We loved her, and because we loved her, we started thinking she owed us the truth about herself. Didn't she realize that coming clean on her humble beginnings would only make her story more inspirational and render her more heroic? Didn't she realize that if she admitted she was 100 percent self-made we would love her even more?

But a basic college course in psychology will tell you that's not how it works for the self-invented. Chanel may have prevaricated about her childhood for the perverse fun of being contrary, but she also knew instinctively that she needed to believe she came from better circumstances in order to continue being who she was; she needed to believe in her bones that she was worth the money and respect she commanded.

Faulkner said, "The past isn't dead, it isn't even the past," and nowhere is this more true than for the self-made. In our modern collective hysteria over celebrity—and the superpower we believe it confers—we completely forget that every single day every one of us still has to get up in the morning, get dressed, brush our teeth, and slay our particular dragons.

Self-invention is an act of the imagination, the ongoing writing of an enormous never-ending novel in which you are the protagonist. It's not a makeover, a new hair color, a new wardrobe, or even a week-long wellness vacation in the desert. It requires a rugged determination, and sometimes some unflattering desperation. It means doing whatever it takes—including sprucing up our personal history, the autobiographical equivalent of amending the soil before planting the roses. Believing our DNA is infused with, for example, a feisty clan of iconoclastic Celtic rogues and storytellers, as opposed to three generations of town drunks, may make the difference between becoming the next James Cameron or inheriting our father's stool at the Stumble Inn. History, as we know, is written by the winners, and this goes for personal history as well.

Tips for Refashioning Your Past à la Chanel

Blame all the bad behavior of your forebears on passion.
Chanel insisted that even though her father Albert appeared to be an irresponsible philanderer, he was really a loving husband who made her mother very happy. She claimed that her parents were deeply, passionately in love. So in love were they, that when her mother went into labor, she flew to Albert's side for a romantic assignation. But the baby wouldn't wait, and the poorhouse just happened to be on the way. The implication is that had Jeanne taken a different route, or left a little earlier or a little later, she might have given birth at a better address. The poorhouse nuns were so kind to Jeanne, she graciously honored their generosity by naming her daughter Gabrielle Bonheur, after the one who attended her labor and delivery. In some versions of this tale, there was no poorhouse and no nuns, instead she was born in Saumur, in the home of some people Jeanne had met on the train. Now that's hospitality.

Identify with the most glamorous member of your family.
Chanel was a daddy's girl, and like all daddy's girls since Athena sprang fully formed from the head of Zeus, she defended Albert even when he didn't deserve it. She claimed variously that her father was

not a peddler, but a man who speculated on wines (much sexier). Or she would demur and say she had no idea what he did. She claimed he adored her and gave her the nickname Coco when she was a wee babe (her biographers agree that her nickname came from one of two of her greatest hits during her caf'conc days, "Qui qu'a vu Coco" about a distressed Parisian girl who'd lost her dog, or "Ko-ko-ri-ko," which had to do with the travails of a rooster).

She even took Albert's side in his abandonment of his children. It was nothing more than bad luck, pure and simple, that his wife died on him when she did. There was nothing for him to do than— what else?—go to America to seek his fortune. She told the other girls at the orphanage that he would be coming back from America any day.* Decades later, she told her friends that he'd had no choice. What was a man so young, dashing, and charming to do? Chanel said repeatedly that had she been him, she would have done the same thing. This was probably the truth.

Rename the people who humiliated you.

Chanel had a shockingly bad temper (sometimes she would get so angry she would clench her fists and jump up and down), and it must have infuriated her to be stuck in an orphanage when technically she was not an orphan. Her father was alive and well and in America making a fortune.

There was no evidence Albert Chanel ever left France. When they were all adults, Lucien Chanel, Coco's brother, tried to track down their father and discovered him living in the north with a much younger woman; Albert invited Lucien to stay with them, then disappeared again when Lucien arrived.

For her entire life Chanel refused to acknowledge she'd ever even set foot in an orphanage. Her thinking may have gone like this: I was not an orphan, therefore I was not raised in an orphanage. That being the case, I was not raised by nuns (horrors) but by a pair of strict nun-like aunts.

The "aunts" were austere, yet earthy and wise in their provincialism. They insisted Chanel wear a uniform for her homeschooling. On the same day every year the aunts removed the household linens from their cupboards and re-ironed them. Their floors were gleaming, their discipline extreme. The aunts taught Chanel to sew. "If I have a certain preference for order, for comfort, for having things done right, for chests filled with linens that smell good . . . I owe it to my aunts."

The nonexistent aunts came in very handy over the years. The years between the orphanage and the establishment of her shop on Rue Cambon were of no interest to Chanel. She wasn't keen on remembering her salad days as a shopgirl; so instead she dragged out the aunts. *These* aunts owned pastures, which they leased to the local cavalry. There the horses would be turned out to recuperate, and Chanel would catch them and gallop them bareback across the fields, her long black hair whipping in the wind! Very romantic. There were also some real aunts, and it didn't help matters that one of them, her Aunt Louise, actually did have a hand in teaching her how to sew. We think.

Embrace your region.

Chanel may have had no use for her family, but she was happy to attribute much of her success to her no-nonsense provincial roots.

To be from the Auvergne was to be a natural salesman, to create in people a need for what you had to offer, to be shrewd, calculating, and also charming.

The Auvergne has an ancient and bloody history. It was occupied variously by the Visigoths, the Franks, and in the eleventh century the First Crusade was organized there, at the Council of Clermont. Anne Rice's fictional vampire Lestat de Lioncourt was born there. Auvergnates are considered tough, frugal, and strong of character; being an Auvergnate was a little like being an American Midwesterner, with the street sense of a New Yorker.

To embrace the characteristics of your region is a way of belonging to a large family, without the obligations. It's a way of belonging, without being expected to show up for Thanksgiving.

It should be noted that technically Chanel was from Saumur, a town in the Maine-et-Loire district, and not from the Auvergne, although her mother was.

Cast yourself as the romantic heroine.

Chanel was not well educated, but she had a brilliant-to-the-point-of-uncanny knack for absorbing everything that came her way. One of her favorite novelists was Gyp (aka Sybille Gabrielle Marie-Antoinette de Riquetti de Mirabeau, Comtesse de Martel), whose romances were serialized in the local papers. Ardent fans cut out each installment and made "books" from the clippings.

Chanel had a real aunt and uncle (Aunt Louise and Uncle Paul) whom she would occasionally visit on the holidays; there she would pore over Aunt Louise's clipping books of Gyp's latest romance. Sometimes she snuck the books back to the orphanage, where she would read them in secret. Gyp's fashion-intensive stories starred flirtatious tomboys who nevertheless enjoyed wearing fancy gowns and lush petticoats—Chanel's personality in a nutshell.

Chanel had several things going for her—not the least of which was the sting of necessity, which forced her to inventory her modest advantages and figure out how to leverage them. Her list was short but would serve her in good stead for the rest of her life:

a. Her looks.

b. Her mind, including her powers of observation.

c. Her ability to gallop a horse through the forest.

In 1900, several years before Chanel met Balsan, the best-selling novel *Claudine at School* (*Claudine à l'école*) was published by famous wit and music critic Henri Gauthier-Villars, who wrote under the pen name Willy. Claudine was a fifteen-year-old provincial school girl—brash, mouthy, and beguiling, the first modern teenager. Her adventures were catalogued in sensationally successful installments (they were the *Harry Potter* books of their day) that inspired a hilarious assortment of ancillary products: Claudine soap, Claudine perfume, Claudine cigars, and an entire Claudine uniform. As literary legend has it, Willy had nothing to do with the Claudine books, other than reaping their tremendous profits. Hoping to help his young wife,

Sidonie-Gabrielle Colette, realize her own writing ambitions, he would lock her in a room every morning and refuse to let her out until she'd written enough Claudine-filled pages for the day (appalling as it may sound, most writers I know would welcome such enforced captivity). Eventually, Sidonie came out as the real author, dumped her husband for the usual reasons, became a music-hall performer, adopted the pen name Colette, and created history. Later in their lives, Colette and Chanel would enjoy an odd couple-ish friendship. Chanel thought Colette was too undisciplined and fat; Colette found Chanel to be waspish and severe.

Even if Chanel hadn't strenuously objected to being thought of as kept (who knows how she rationalized her situation to herself—maybe she viewed her time under Balsan's wing as sort of an extended retreat, where in exchange for her favors she was given a lot of unstructured time to figure out her life), she was a misfit, an odd duck amid swans. She was twenty-five and looked fifteen, flat chested, thin hipped, scrappy. She was a Claudine. Her unusual beauty was a few years short of being all the rage, and she looked completely ridiculous in the upholstered finery of the day. Whether Balsan and the horsey set at Royallieu were familiar with the Claudine books is doubtful; the only thing they read on a regular basis was the racing pages. It's probably also safe to assume that the demands of breeding, breaking, training, racing, and selling horses consumed them to the exclusion of most everything else aside from throwing parties. Still, the Claudine aesthetic was in the air. It was the look of the future, if not the present. Chanel was a curiosity, and she knew it.

The women who accompanied the racehorse owners, aristocratic breeders, polo players, and famous jockeys who came to Royallieu for the house parties and costume balls were renegade women—longtime mistresses, popular courtesans, gold diggers, and other floozies du jour, including the occasional actress at loose ends. Some of them were considered great beauties (including Émilienne d'Alençon, whose image you can still catch on the enduringly popular Folies Bergère posters, the kind often hung in the ladies' rooms of fashionable cafes). They were soft and curvy, padded just about every place a woman could be padded, pouffy of lip, doughy of arm, indolent, sloe-eyed, bovine.

Chanel was fascinated and unnerved by them. Sometimes she ate in the kitchen to avoid being compared with them. Near the end of her life, she remembered those cocottes, those preferred, fashionable women: "All those ladies were badly dressed, in their body armor, with their bosoms out, their behinds jutting out too, bound in at the waist until they were almost cut in two. They were dressed to the teeth . . . still, I didn't think the cocottes were all that bad. I thought they were very pretty with their hats broader than their shoulders, and their big, heavily made-up eyes. They were sumptuous."

Chanel was not sumptuous, and she looked completely ridiculous in the finery of the day—the blouses made fussy with appliqués; insertions of lace, pleats, pin tucks, and trim; the long-trained trumpet flower–shaped skirts; the S-bend corsets (so named because when tightly laced they forced the hips back and the mono-boob forward, making you look like a pigeon); the gold, pearl, or diamond encrusted stomacher;* the fur-trimmed capes and oversize muffs; the pelisses** and mantelets;*** the embroidered silk gloves and lace encrusted parasols. And of course, the hats.

There was no way to compete with the ladies of turf society, so Chanel leveled the playing field by changing it—to the stables. She spent most of her days riding Balsan's thoroughbreds. She rode daily, in the blazing heat that turned the trails to dust and the muddy slop of winter. She became famous at the barn for working young horses in training, the problem mounts that gave the trainers fits and that the jockeys avoided when they could. No woman in Balsan's life ever involved herself in his world in this way, and so she made a name for herself.

She became famous for throwing herself onto the back of a two-year-old stallion and thundering off into the woods, which kept Balsan amused and impressed his friends. He liked to show off her ability to ride astride—something ladies didn't do at the time—and took her foxhunting with a bunch of the boys. At the height of her glory, Chanel was always happy to pass on the secret to riding well—pretend you're a man with a pair of testicles between you and the saddle and ". . . under no circumstances can you put an ounce of

---

*A decorative panel, usually triangular, that extends from the neckline to the waist, covering a woman's bodice. May be boned or part of a corset.
** A three-quarter-length coat, sometimes with an attached shoulder cape.
*** A short coat with weird sleeves.

weight on them." D'Alençon, it was said, didn't even know what the stables looked like. She refused Balsan's offers to visit because she was afraid of getting her shoes dirty.

All this is a way of proving to you that Chanel didn't start out with a mission statement, nor a corporate vision, nor a roadmap for success, nor a timeline for achieving her goals, nor an action item list, nor any of those other high-falutin' concepts we associate with megamodern multinational success stories.

But her first big moves, the ones that would propel her to the next level, were made out of pure necessity. She loved her little suits, a variation on the same thing she wore when she was a teenager, because the extravagant clothes that were in vogue did not suit her and they set her aside from the run-of-the-mill kept woman, who was always overdone. And let's not forget the cost. Balsan was wealthy, but he was neither a prince nor a duke. Everything he had he put into his stables. Many of Chanel's early pieces were designed in defiance of what she knew she could never have.

Likewise Chanel turned herself into a formidable horsewoman, in part because it was the only thing at hand that could charm the powerful men in her life who otherwise might have lost interest in a girl with apparently so little to offer. If the men had all been mad golfers, or passionate about their cheese making, who knows what would have happened to her.

The famously poetic yet inarticulate Bob Dylan, another master of self-invention, tried once to explain his success: "I was just doing what I could with what I had where I was." He was not just making it up as he went along; he was also using everything he stumbled upon. He was both weaving the rope and climbing it at the same time.

And so was Coco Chanel.

3

ON FEARLESSNESS

*"The most courageous act is still to think
for yourself. Aloud."*

'd planned to segue from the idea that Coco Chanel's revolutionary style was a gut response to not fitting in with the cool kids
at Royallieu, to a discussion of her remarkable audacity. But I can't
seem to spur myself on when instinct tells me that a more pressing
issue looms—namely, how I might get my hands on some Chanel.

I find it slightly strange to be writing about Chanel's life when
my sole involvement with haute couture consists of being the granddaughter of Luna of California, who designed clothes primarily for
the wives of movie moguls in Los Angeles in the 1950s (her styles
were influenced by Dior—alas, the man whose post–World War II,
impractical big-skirted excesses were the call to arms Chanel needed
to drag herself out of retirement like an aging superhero) and buying
a fake Marc Jacobs bag ten years ago in Chelsea, before we were all
set straight on the evils of purchasing knockoffs. I don't own a pair
of Chanel sunglasses, or even a pair of sparkly ten-dollar interlocking
rhinestone Cs, available for purchase at every low-end jewelry store
in the known world.

I fell for Chanel in the spring of 1979, upon glimpsing the sleeve-less black sheath worn by Audrey Hepburn in *Breakfast at Tiffany's*. (The cigarette holder! The gloves! The tiara!) Watching the movie was part of an undergraduate writing assignment in which we were to compare and contrast a novel with its film adaptation. I chose *BAT* because Truman Capote's novel was very short (I was also taking organic chemistry that semester) and the movie starred Audrey Hepburn, who'd also starred as a blind lady being terrorized by a homicidal maniac in *Wait Until Dark,* which had scared the living crap out of me when I'd snuck into a theater to watch it in grade school. Stumbling upon Hepburn's gorgeous black dress was a happy accident. I argued unconvincingly in my paper that the costumes were more memorable than the script. My English teacher accused me of being both off-topic and cavalier. But I was right. The little black dress stole the show, even though it was designed by Hubert de Givenchy. I checked out a book about Givenchy from the college library and discovered within a chapter or two that all roads lead to Chanel.

But they don't lead to owning a little black dress. I would never have a reason for owning a little black dress, designed by anyone. The only dress-up affairs I ever seem to attend are weddings. And the last time I checked, wearing black to a wedding was still in bad taste, although perhaps it's like wearing white after Labor Day, a tradition left over from the era when ladies wore gloves. The day may come when I do receive an invitation to a black-tie fund-raiser, or to be a seat saver at the Oscars, but at the moment I have absolutely no use for a black dress (aside from the psychological benefit gained from knowing I am stylish enough to have a black dress in the closet, hanging at the ready).

Regardless, fashion mavens insist that spending thousands for a little black dress is a good investment. It doesn't seem to matter what the little black dress looks like—that because you can accurately apply the adjectives *little* and *black*, the dress is automatically timeless, even if it does have ruched bell sleeves of beaded Chantilly lace that evoke the cheesiest fashion moments of the 1980s. Come to think of it, the same fashion folk have advised me that clothes from the 1980s are now considered vintage. Can timeless also be vintage? I thought vintage was old-but-still-cool-but-in-an-ironic-fashion, and timeless was supposed to look as if it was designed and manufactured yesterday.

After careful thought (I'm wary about dropping a lot of money on clothes I may never wear, unlike my habit of treating amazon.com like a lending library, haphazardly ordering up armfuls of books I'm unlikely to read), I decided I could do with a Chanel jacket. I sat with the idea for several days. It would mean dipping into savings. I told myself it would be an investment, which is more than can be said for my paltry near-zero interest Bank of America savings account.

One Sunday morning, still in my bathrobe, I logged onto eBay. I haven't had a good experience with eBay. I went through an old movie poster phase some years ago and purchased what I thought was an original one-sheet from *Breakfast at Tiffany's*. It was a steal, and no one bid against me! My "poster" turned out to be a very nice 8x10-inch color Xerox. It was my fault. I was such a newbie. I hadn't checked the seller's reviews; it turns out I wasn't the only one who'd been hosed. But I was willing to try again.

There were 217 Chanel jackets on offer. Instantly I was presented with the Chanel-Chanel versus the Lagerfeld-Chanel dilemma. In Lagerfeld's ready-to-wear collections there are always three or four jackets that are reliably beautiful, chic, and normal-enough looking that you wouldn't have to overhaul your entire life, look, and personal philosophy in order to throw one on. To own a Chanel-Chanel piece would be to own a piece of history, but alas, I don't have a collector gene in my body—my largest and only collection is a pair of ashtrays from famous French restaurants, one from La Coupole and one from Les Deux Magots, stolen straight from their adorable tables before they had in-cafe boutiques—and so I can't whip up enough enthusiasm (at least at the moment; stay tuned) to care about what it might mean to own Chanel-Chanel.

At first I thought any Chanel jacket in my price range (three figures is better than four) and size would satisfy me, but I realized fairly quickly that a Chanel jacket could still be unflattering. I didn't want anything that buttoned up to the neck (too Sergeant Pepper), nor anything too overtly blazer-ish (too Realtor Lady). Within minutes of scrolling through the listings, I realized I had a Goldilocks situation on my hands. This jacket was too small; *this* jacket was too small and too expensive; *this* jacket was the right size, but was not in a color that flattered me or that I particularly liked; *this* jacket was the right size, but was from the 08P collection and therefore both not the right size (anything from any P collection could not possibly be the right size) and not interesting, especially for $5,065. Then I developed a headache that throbbed ominously over one eyeball socket, the same one I get when doing the taxes.

Which brings up another issue—and as soon as I articulate it here, I'm going to lob it back to the farthest, darkest, least-visited corner of my mind, like a bridegroom who collected phone numbers at his bachelor party: What am I doing? What in the *hell* am I doing? Just because I adore Chanel, am in awe of her, wish to emulate her style, grit, spunk, and wit (the self-involved, back-biting, Nazi-sympathizing part, not so much), I have no business assuming I have the means to own any Chanel.

I am the average consumer: I have several credit cards in my wallet. One of them magically summons forth a monthly magazine whose sole purpose is to remind me that there are stupendously expensive things to buy out there, luxury items that would have fallen off my radar had they ever been on it.

The day before, I'd received one card's annual style guide. Flipping through it I came upon an ad for $19,000 Roberto Coin gold and enamel chokers and a report on Donna Karan's new "affordable" bag, priced at $2,200 (we live in troubled economic times). There were some beautifully designed chairs that you would never want to sit on, running about five grand each. There were the usual Armani/Louis Vuitton/Rolex/Four Seasons ads. I thought, okay, I'm not a complete tool, I do own a black wool Armani coat (purchased at the Barney's warehouse sale) and a Tudor watch (manufactured by Rolex). I was a guest of the Four Seasons Maldives for ten days (while on assignment for a magazine), and not once did the staff treat me as someone who'd wandered onto the property hoping to use the restroom or take an unauthorized dip in the pool.

Then I flipped to the Netjets ad, featuring Bill Gates and Warren Buffett on a Boeing business jet. The richest man on Earth and the first runner-up (Carlos Slim, the Mexican cell phone magnet, might be richer than Bill Gates but he was not featured in the ad). The guys were in their shirtsleeves, slouched on a corduroy sectional like the one we have in our TV room. The props on the table before them included playing cards and a bowl of jelly beans, proving that what we've known all along is true: They're just a pair of gin-rummy-playing, jelly-bean-eating fools. I turned the page. When I came upon the update on this year's polo season in Buenos Aires—the most expensive sport in the world—the wake-up call was not far behind. Who was I *kidding* with this Chanel business?

There's nothing more curmudgeonly than bringing up real-world concerns in a book that concerns itself with style and fashion. But as of this writing, I have, among other things, a daughter applying for college next year and the usual paltry self-employed person's health insurance (read: a hospital stay for more than several hours spells financial ruin), and then, of course there is the colossal credit crunch/stock market/sub-prime disaster, which doesn't affect me much, really, since my IRA tanked ten years ago, as the bulk of it was invested in Pets.com or something.

Anyway, the point is this: Designers who work for houses that produce low-end pieces that still cost more than a mortgage payment—forget couture—often try to reassure the Gap-bejeaned consumer that style isn't about money. Perhaps what they mean to say is that being stylish is worth the cost, that the money shouldn't concern you. Otherwise they're just feeding us all a line of bull. An Hermès crocodile Kelly bag and a black Chanel evening dress of embroidered lace are beautiful objects perfectly made from high-quality materials. Cheap knockoffs are just that. They pucker, pinch, rise up, droop, and itch, then disintegrate in the machine the second time you wash them. Style has always been about money, and it always will be.

Still.

From the perspective of someone who is able to overcome her fears only sporadically through a combination of deep yogic breathing and self-talk, the strong, unrelenting heartbeat of Chanel's courage alone is enough to qualify her for beatification, St. Coco, Patron Saint of Jersey (the fabric, not the island).

After Chanel realized she could more or less single-handedly (let's not forget her assistants—she could not have done what she did without the little people) overthrow the institution of the twenty-pound platter hat with her saucy department-store boaters, she decided she could do the same for all of women's fashion. *Pourquoi pas?* Why not? It was the same principle, only on a larger scale. She was like a warrior queen who invaded a little country as practice for attacking a larger one.

It was the summer of 1914, the uneasy first summer of the first World War, and everyone who could fled Paris for Deauville, a posh resort on the northeastern coast of France, known for its racetrack, Grand casino, and grand hotels. Chanel (with the backing of her new lover, Boy Capel) opened Chanel Modes on the main drag between the most luxurious hotel in town and the Grand Casino, and there she started selling little skirts and fetching cardigans.

A lucky heat wave in July, and that being-on-holiday-so-what-the-hell feeling that in our times manifests itself as a willingness to stop at the market on the way home from the beach in a sarong, sent fashionable society ladies (with fabulous rich-lady names like Princess Baba de Faucigny-Lucinge and Pauline de Saint-Sauveur) into Coco's shop for her light, comfy pieces, which would soon be known as sportswear, even though the only "sport" women engaged in then was the occasional slow bike ride, promenading between shops and motoring.

The creation of the fetching cardigan has its own equally fetching Chanelore behind it. One day Chanel was tromping around the barn/at the races or strolling along the beach and asked to borrow boyfriend Capel's pullover. This was the kind of relationship they had, intimate and chummy. She could ask to borrow his clothes and Capel, an iconoclast in his own right, thought nothing of it. But the pullover ... what a nuisance to haul this thing on over her head—one presumes she had to remove her nervy little straw boater first—and so she simply took a pair of scissors, cut the pullover up the middle, belted it, and Bob's your uncle. How the shears and belt miraculously appeared at the barn/track/shore is one of those charming Chanelian mysteries that we faithful simply accept. It supports the observation of her friend Paul Morand (novelist, diplomat, modernist, friend of Proust) that she "built her wardrobe in response to her needs, just the way Robinson Crusoe built his hut."

It took pluck to introduce easy-to-wear clothes during an era when "clothes" and "easy-to-wear" had never yet appeared together in a sentence. At the end of the Belle Époque, the S-bend corset was out, but the long-line corset, looser laced but extending to the knees(!) for a slimming effect, was in, and women's clothes were still a cross between costume and armor. Ladies dressed every morning in a woman disguise, in clothes designed to aggressively suggest femininity while at the same time hiding the female shape lurking beneath.

So Chanel, the young milliner who still scrubbed with the same no-nonsense soap the nuns used at the orphanage, with one cheeky, well-received concept under her belt (simplify!), decided to expand. She decided rather than disguising women as women, it was time to create clothes that allowed the ladies to work it.

Historians differ on how she came to take this giant step forward. Some say she was innocently putting one delicate foot in front of the other, and moving from hats into clothing was the next obvious thing; others believe she was a crafty businesswoman with a master plan hatched—I'm guessing—during all those idle hours at Royallieu while she was helping Étienne Balsan's grooms tend the thoroughbreds (as anyone who has horses in her life knows, for every hour in the saddle there are hours and hours of cooling down, bathing, brushing, hoof picking, etc.). I've decided to believe the latter, that she was a crafty faux Auvergnate bent on conquering the world in her own way, as opposed to a darling wee thing that simple fell into monumental, world-changing success.

Anyway, it was her big idea at a time when she needed a big idea. Chanel always looked young and passed herself off as younger. If she could have continued to pass herself off as eighteen indefinitely, she would have. In 1914 she was thirty-one, a few years past the age when women who were neither wives nor mothers were written off as "redundant." In this way things haven't changed much. Or rather they changed about forty years ago, when it was thought that a woman needed a man like a fish needed a bicycle, and then they changed back. To be thirty-one and unmarried is the same tragedy now as it was a hundred years ago, back in the days when driving was considered a sport. At any rate, Chanel's fate wasn't yet guaranteed. Just because she had a successful hat business, that didn't mean she wouldn't be thrown over by Capel (as she eventually was) and left husbandless, family-less, penniless.

❋❋❋

Most of us, when we land upon a great idea, a lifesaving idea, immediately turn it into our baby. And like our real-life babies, we only want the best for it. We love it. We coddle it. It's our great idea, and who knows when we might have another one! We want to implement it at the right time with the best materials possible. We want the stars to be right.

But Chanel's chutzpah dictated the opposite. She was going to reinvent the female wardrobe, and she was going to do it now with whatever was at hand. And what was at hand was jersey, then thought of as the cheesiest material possible.

If the world of fabric was high school, jersey was the personality-free, nearly invisible nerd everyone avoided at lunch. Stretchy, clingy, and cheap, it came in colors like beige, medium beige, light beige, and lighter beige. It was the opposite of silk, wool, cashmere, tulle, and other fine fabrics that could, at the very least, hold their own shape.

How did Chanel decide to use this red-headed stepchild of fabrics? The Chanelore differs. Either she got a sensational deal on a lot of jersey from a manufacturer that decided against using it for the menswear for which it was originally made, or else her lease at the Rue Cambon stipulated that she could only make hats, because there was already another dressmaker on the block. As jersey was not something used to make women's clothes, Chanel's early jackets, skirts, and suits were not considered clothing, and therefore did not violate the terms of her lease (I will not attempt to parse the French bureaucratic logic).

If things hadn't worked out so well, Chanel could have easily been dismissed as a whack-a-doo, and her jersey ensembles written off as the crocheted beer hats of the early twentieth century or the disposable paper minidresses in style for a nanosecond during the 1960s.

But Chanel possessed an unswerving faith in her instincts, which included what she believed to be her impeccable taste. And it was (largely) impeccable, because she believed it was. It was sheer nerve. When she launched her line that summer before the war, her dressmaking skills were nearly nonexistent. She knew how to make hats, and she knew how to explain what she wanted to other people (i.e., the women she hired who *did* have actual dressmaking skills).

It's possible that Chanel's pluck was not as unique as it seems. The history of haute couture and luxury goods is populated with designers who were either born in a box by the side of the road, or like Chanel, suffered childhood traumas straight out of Dickens. For every high-born Miuccia Prada* and Pucci,** there is an Armani, who grew up in a small town near Milan that was so aggressively bombed by the allies during World War II that Giorgio lost his entire gang of boyfriends in a single day. On another day, a rifle cartridge he'd found in the street exploded as he was leaning down to have a look. He spent forty days on the burn ward and still bears the scars. Chanel's contemporary, Madeleine Vionnet, "queen of the bias cut," was born dirt poor in Chilleurs-aux-Bois, Loiret. Her family sent her to begin her apprenticeship as a seamstress at age eleven; by eighteen she had already been married and divorced and was working in London hospital as a seamstress, repairing tattered bedding. Louis Vuitton came from a family of farmers in the foothills of the French Alps; he left

---

Doctor of political science, member of the Italian Communist Party, and former mime.

**Also known as the Marquese di Barsento, born to one of Italy's oldest and most noble families; also the recipient of a skiing scholarship from Reed College, where he earned his M.A. in 1937.*

home at age thirteen for Paris and worked as a stable boy until he was able to apprentice himself to a trunk maker. In 1854, with nothing more than his good ideas as to how a fine trunk should be built, he opened his first shop on the Rue des Capucines. Thierry Hermès was orphaned at fifteen, after his parents and siblings died of various diseases during the Napoleonic Wars. He wandered a bit before settling in Normandy, the heart of French horse country, where he learned to make carriage harnesses. In 1837 he opened his own shop in Paris (not far from Vuitton's) and proceeded to make the most exquisite harnesses, saddles, and eventually, yes, handbags, on Earth.

It's tempting to think that the gene for the courage to impose one's vision of beauty on the world is located .on the chromosome that also determines the ability to create a simple, beautiful object (a bag, a hat, a dress) for which people the world over will pay staggering amounts of money.

Chanel's biographers have surmised that she was able to stick her neck out the way she did because she had nothing to lose, meaning she had no family, no husband, no name, and no money. The other thing she had was no wiggle room. Had her business tanked, she would have lost the patronage of Balsan and Capel, both of whom had absolutely no obligation to underwrite her or her shop. Unlike Blanche Dubois, she was not relying on the kindness of strangers, but on the kindness of *businessmen,* a far riskier proposition.

The moral of the "Using Jersey When Good Sense Would Dictate Using Wool or Something More Sensible" story is twofold. First, when it comes to going with your gut and making the big, bold, seemingly outlandish move, doing so from a precarious position in life is not just a good idea, it's the *best* idea. The very precariousness can, in fact, be a source of strength. Chanel wasn't about to wait to launch her big idea; on the eve of war, in a relative backwater town (Deauville was chic, but it was hardly Paris), modern fashion was born.

Perhaps it's not that unusual to exhibit courage in the course of finding our mètier. In becoming an attorney, a professor, a web designer, a hair stylist, there are challenges that must be met, doors through which you must step to get to the next level. There are crossroads, required leaps of faith, and moments when you need a new idea (jersey!), and thin air is the place you're forced to look for it.

But Chanel was fearless on another front. For the length of her long life, she said what she thought. In case this doesn't strike you as such a huge achievement, consider the cottage industry of bestselling books about the apparent inability of women to speak up, to negotiate, to press on with their ideas when they feel they're not being heard. "The Daily Asker" is a popular blog, wherein the blogger has set herself the goal of asking for something every day. Yes, women can cry and women can rage, but even now, we still struggle with just saying what's on our minds.

Chanel was not just a straight talker, she was a back talker, a woman who embraced her own churlishness. One of the cares she lost when she decided to be someone and not something was that of talking around her real thoughts and feelings, so as not to offend. Really, she couldn't give a damn. Bring it on.

Stendhal (author of *The Red and the Black*, and also ahead of his time) famously observed that the way to offend a Parisian was to call her kind. On this front there is no chance of offending Mademoiselle Chanel. She could be ruthless in her honesty and often downright mean. Unlike most American women she was never tempted to channel her inner, crowd-pleasing Labrador retriever. While she was a masterful flirt, she never felt the need to be kittenish in order to compensate for her wealth and fame.

Once, during the end of the 1920s when Chanel was the queen of Paris chic, after she'd created the famous black dress and after the massive L' Exposition des Arts Decoratifs et Industriels Modernes, where rival Paul Poiret had torpedoed what was left of his brilliant and erratic career by showing opulent floor-length gowns in silver, lamé, velvet taffeta, and chiffon, totally missing the "modern" aspect of the exposition, Chanel ran into him on the sidewalk. Poor Poiret had not just fallen out of favor, his finances were also in ruins. In addition to the expensive, out-of-style gowns he'd just shown at the Expo, he'd insisted on exhibiting them on a trio of electrically lit river barges, which cost the moon. Before this, in an effort to shore up his reputation and combat Chanel's stubborn devotion to plainness, he even created dresses lit from the inside with tiny bulbs. At the risk of sounding Seussian: He was down, she was up. He was over, she was on top. When she met him that day on the sidewalk, it would have been nothing for her to have been gracious.

Seeing Chanel in her little black suit with white schoolgirl collar and cuffs, Poiret said sarcastically, "What are you in mourning for, Mademoiselle?"

She said, "For you, dear Monsieur."

Chanel's wit was not gentle but combative; she was Dorothy Parker with a pair of shears. Aside from her basic French disinclination to be agreeable, and her Cinderella complex, she bore the indignity of being a mere dressmaker. Even as she was becoming a success, when her hats were being worn exclusively by major actresses and she expanded her business to include both Biarritz and Paris (by 1917 she had five workrooms; in one workroom sixty seamstresses worked on clothes for Spain alone), she was routinely snubbed by the aristocratic women who were paying astronomical amounts for her clothes. They would spend hours having a fitting at her shop, then the next day pretend she was invisible when they ran into her at the races. This wasn't unusual. Couturiers were considered tradespeople, no better than cabinetmakers and knife sharpeners. Charles Worth, the so-called father of haute couture, would cross the street when he saw a client, so as not to put her in the position of having to ignore him.

Then came Chanel with her neat, fresh clothes and her disinclination to take crap from anyone. She was charming, but she refused to censor herself. She sneered at the husbands of her clients and said, "Those grand dukes were all the same. They were tall and handsome and splendid, but behind it all—nothing; just vodka and the void." Of the increasingly zaftig Colette she said, "Colette preferred two grilled sausages to love." She called Picasso "that Spaniard, with his hat."

The result of all this mouthing off was not what you might expect. Rather than driving people away, Chanel's devotion to thinking for herself, aloud, drew them to her, made her intriguing. She simply did not have the time, the energy, nor the inclination to care what anyone thought of her. Life was serious. She was serious. She defined luxury as liberty (see chapter 12), and stopping to censor herself, to make herself pleasing to others, would be depriving her of luxury. Until she was a very old and very cantankerous old lady, Chanel was beloved. Axel Madsen closes his superb biography of Chanel with a kind, malice-free remark by the sausage-loving Colette, "It is in the secret of her work that we must find this thoughtful conqueror."

Am I suggesting then that we err on the side of being a big 'ol bitch (or in this case a tiny, chic bitch)? Yes I am.

4

ON SURVIVING PASSION

"Great loves too must be endured."

L ike a lot of cultural icons, Chanel's love life was, by our most
cherished love-marriage-baby carriage standards, somewhat
sketchy. She was only *in* love once and never married. While man-
aging to marry is no guarantee that you know a single thing about
the intricacies of loving and being loved, failing to make that final
commitment suggests that somehow you never made it to the big
leagues. If you're a woman, it suggests that something was deeply
wrong with you or, paradoxically, *right* with you; being too successful, too gorgeous, too smart, and too sexy have also been known to
send prospective suitors scampering down the mountainside to less-
challenging romantic terrain.

In addition, there is also no arguing with the deeply entrenched—
if wrongheaded—sentiment that the longer a marriage is, the happier
it is. This is like evaluating the deliciousness of food by its shelf life.
By this logic a head of cabbage is more delectable than a raspberry,
and those molar-cracking candy conversation hearts that are so
popular on Valentine's Day (said to be edible for twenty years) are
sweeter than a chocolate truffle. Chanel said, "I dislike grapefruit and

things grown in cotton-wool. Fruit should be eaten in season." Her philosophy of love was similar.

The romance novel–reading part of Chanel may have wanted to marry, but in the pie chart of her personality, that desire was sliver-size compared to the part that commanded twenty-four hundred forewomen in fifty-six workrooms, created two collections a year, launched a perfume empire, invented the concept of costume jewelry, learned to fly-fish, and bred racehorses, while at all times looking fantastic. Chanel once said, "One marries for security and prestige. I'm not interested in all that." She wasn't interested in all that because she already had all that. Which left her with love for love's sake, i.e., standing on that part of the romantic map where the known world ends and it says "Here be dragons."

Even though we marry largely for love in the Western world, our love lives are still often colored by the need/desire/preference to land a man who can buy us a house on a good street and give us the freedom to quit our jobs when the baby is born (he will also, of course, be in possession of a great sense of humor and a secret abiding love of screwball comedies and whatever else we find irresistible).

Chanel had one great love, and at the risk of sounding like my mother, she should have considered herself lucky; some people (even those who've enjoyed successful marriages) never get any. Chanel and Arthur "Boy" Capel met sometime around 1905. She had been living at Royallieu for several years when the dashing English polo-player, an old friend of Balsan's, showed up one day to look at his horses and was immediately smitten by Chanel. Unlike Balsan, who'd turned a deaf ear to Chanel's ambitions—hadn't he done enough setting her up in her silly hat business?— Capel listened to her. He was intrigued. He was a man of the world, an industrialist from Newcastle, who'd made a small fortune exporting coal and would make an even larger fortune during World War I, supplying the Allies with fuel.

Balsan's friends, and the rest of the landed gentry, found him eccentric for loving work as much as loving leisure. He was handsome and charismatic. Unlike many historic figures who in photographs never look as hot as they were alleged to have been during their day (they're always too fat or too thin or squint grimly into the camera, in desperate need of a stylist), pictures of Capel show him to be sexy, dark haired, and muscular. He brings to mind Colin Farrell or the James McAvoy of *Atonement* (a necessary distinction, since McAvoy was also creepily good at portraying Mr. Tumnus the Faun in *The Chronicles of Narnia: The Lion, the Witch and the Wardrobe*).

As Chanelore has it, Chanel made the switch from Balsan to Capel one evening in the drawing room at Royallieu. The three of them were enjoying their port and Chanel, feeling bold from the wine and Capel's attention, brought up the subject of opening a boutique. She had been making and selling hats from Balsan's Paris apartment, but she wanted to expand her business. Balsan rolled his eyes, so tired was he of her refusal to be happy with what she had. Capel took him to task, arguing for Chanel's talent, her brilliant mind, her ability to make a business work. He was in love.

In some French and utterly urbane manner, the change was negotiated. Some accounts say that Balsan relinquished his interest in her on the day two of his horses won races at Le Tremblay and he was feeling expansive, and some report that he suddenly conceived a need to take himself to Argentina for some polo-related business, and while he was gone Chanel left for Paris with Capel (in this version there is a symbolic bag of lemons that Balsan brings back for Chanel, and when she opens the bag they are all rotten).

In Chanel's own version of events, there was no booze-fueled drawing-room barter. Instead Balsan, hoping to allay some of her boredom, invited her to a foxhunt in Pau, in the high meadows of the Pyrenees, near the Spanish border. There she met and fell head over heels with Capel, who was gorgeous in his red hunting jacket astride his high-spirited Arabian. He was equally smitten. They kept stealing away from the hunt, galloping through the emerald green hills; jumping the clear, rushing streams; and of course, falling in love. At the end of the trip, Chanel learned the time Capel's train was leaving from the station and left everything behind to wait for him there, not knowing whether or not he would accept her. When he saw her, he opened his arms and their bond was sealed.*

The young lovers moved to Paris, where they lived quietly on the elegant Avenue Gabriel, not far from the Champs-Elysées. For the first time in her life, Chanel was in the love shack, that near-mythic place where the colors are brighter, the food tastes better, people are more intriguing, and damn if it isn't just great to be alive! She'd found

---

The people who knew Chanel well rolled their eyes at the melodrama; the woman who thought you were doomed if you left the house without perfume would never hop on a train without a suitcase.

a man who was both attracted to her unusual beauty and her quick mind, who saw her as more than a *petite amie*. And he'd found a woman who enchanted him: She was fierce, funny, and possessed that aristocratic profile (as we shall see, he was rather too impressed with the aristocracy).

Capel worked a lot, but in the evenings he took Chanel to the Opera and Maxims. She was dazzled, but shy. Chanel would become the global symbol of Parisian chic, but at twenty-seven she was still a provincial orphan whose claim to fame was working the well-bred horses of a well-bred man and some sweet, unusual hats.

Chanel didn't open her shop on the Rue Cambon immediately. For all Boy's belief in her vision and brilliance, he was busy making his own millions, and Coco spent a good year sitting in the apartment polishing her nails. He finally made the move to underwrite her shop when he realized her boredom with hat-making threatened their happiness. He told his friend Elisabeth de Gramont (aka the Duchess of Clermont-Tonnere, friend of Proust, and lover of literary salon dominatrix Natalie Clifford Barney) that "it isn't difficult to make hearts beat in unison, but the hands on two different watches were another problem."

In 1910 Chanel Modes opened at 21, Rue Cambon,* and by 1912 Coco began selling sweaters, skirts, and a few dresses. Socialite Suzanne Orlandi was the first woman to wear a Chanel original—a black velvet dress with a simple, stark white petal collar. In the summer of 1913, Capel financed the opening of her shop in Deauville.

---

* *In 1928 Chanel moved her fashion house to 31, Rue Cambon, where it occupied three floors.*

Georges Goursat Sem, the caricaturist of the moment, drew a picture of Chanel in a pink dress, a green and white striped hat box dangling from the crook of her elbow, embraced by Capel, depicted as a centaur in a black polo vest, who's just scooped up one of her pert hats and balances it on the top of his mallet. They were the Brad and Angelina of the day, without all the children.

Could they have married and lived happily ever after? Capel was an enthusiastic philanderer, but Chanel wasn't the jealous type. She considered his fooling around to be a disgusting habit on par with avid cuticle chewing. She adored him, considered him to be not just her lover but also her family.

The failure of the relationship was Shakespearean: As soon as she started turning a profit, she paid him back. She couldn't help it; her instinct for good business overrode all other instincts, including the one that says most conventional men need women who need *them*. The day she handed him the cash she said, "I'll know I really love you when I no longer need you." His initial reaction was jealousy, but over time, without either of them quite realizing it was happening, their bond began to erode. He worked; she worked.

Capel's ambition always guided his behavior. As enamored as he was by Chanel and what she was becoming, he needed a more traditional wife in order to enhance his station; he could only gain a foothold in the aristocracy by marrying one of its daughters.

In the winter of 1918, Capel became engaged to the young, uninteresting (by Chanel's standards) Diana Lister Wyndham. The rumor mill suggested that after Chanel realized Capel would never marry her, she engineered his engagement to someone who would never pose a threat, a girl who would fulfill his ambitions without touching his heart. Chanel and Capel continued to see each other after his wedding.

Several days before Christmas, 1919, on his way from Paris to Cannes, the tire in Capel's new car blew, and he was killed in the fiery crash that followed. He was thirty-eight years old. A mutual friend arrived in the middle of the night to deliver the news. Chanel dressed and ordered the car around. Her instincts were always tactile; she needed to touch something to know it. The crash had happened on the road from St. Raphael. Chanel and her driver arrived at the site just as the sun was coming up over the Cote d'Azur. No one had moved the wreckage. Chanel got out and placed her hands on the fender. Then she sat down and cried.

After Capel's death Chanel ordered the furniture in her bedroom suite to be covered in black fabric. She ordered black sheets for the bed and black curtains for the windows. She was determined to give herself over to her mourning as completely as possible. But the day the redecorating was done, she discovered she couldn't possibly sleep in such a depressing place. She was, in the end, a peasant with a practical streak; the all-black suite was too hysterical and over the top. She had Joseph, her butler, make her bed up in another room.

Diana Wyndham was the official widow, but Chanel felt like one. Capel had not only loved her, be believed in her talent when no one else did. Chanel may have had a hand in inventing the modern woman, but she was the product of an era when women had two options: become a wife or become a courtesan. Capel had loved her both as a woman and as an individual who had something to offer. He launched her and respected her enough to accept her money when it came time to repay his investment. She would never see the likes of him again. To console herself she made the widowed Madame Capel (who eventually remarried and became Countess of Westmoreland) her client.

From then on her attitude toward love changed. She still rhapsodized about amour—it was part of her cultural credo as a French woman—but men became something of a hobby, like the racehorses. They engaged her attention. They amused her. They provided companionship. There was sex, of course, but never again did she experience the skydive of love.

The wags in the local papers used to call Chanel "the woman who forces her heart to remain silent." Her heart wasn't silent, exactly. After the death of Capel she was just less interested in the hymn of its desires. Which is not to say she wasn't interested in men. The champions in her stable would include the following:

Grand Duke Dmitri Pavlovitch
Infatuation, diversion, and friend
1920-1923

Pavlovitch was a professional impoverished aristocrat eight years Chanel's junior. She met him in Biarritz after the collapse of Tsarist Russia in 1917. Tall, blond, and handsome, he was the first cousin of Czar Nicholas II and one of three conspirators involved in the assassination of Rasputin (the Grand Duke poisoned the cake). He was an avid gambler and a teller of charming tales straight out of Tolstoy. He gave Chanel Romanov pearls and enough Slavic charm to last her a lifetime. She loved his penniless, inbred sense of luxury; he loved her pennies and acquired sense of luxury. Their affair ended because she rued his lack of substance. He eventually moved to Palm Beach, Florida, where he became a champagne salesman.

Hugh Richard Arthur Grosvenor, Second Duke of Westminster, aka Bendor
Lover and appropriate match
1925–1930
The Duke of Westminster was the richest man in the world. What's not to love? Chanel met Bendor in Monte Carlo at the height of her celebrity. She loved the gentle, uncomplicated sportsman in him, the childlike personality that resulted from his never knowing how much anything cost; he loved her because she was an exotic beast, the "self-made" woman. He also approved of her horsemanship.* He wooed her with uncut fist-size sapphires nestled in crates of hothouse vegetables grown on his Gothic country estate (which took a full day to travel across, by car) and delivered to Paris on one occasion by the Prince of Wales, whom Chanel mistook as a delivery boy. He ordered his shoelaces ironed every day by his valet, and once offered the strapped-for-

---

Clearly, the greatest life lesson in this book is that knowing how to ride a horse will never fail to impress.

cash poet Jean Cocteau a job writing the biography of his dogs. From all appearances Chanel and the Duke seemed to be a match made in midlife Heaven (She was forty-two, he was forty-six), as people assumed that only a man richer than Chanel could tolerate her greatness. He taught her how to fly-fish, for which she developed a mad passion, and took her for long Mediterranean cruises on his yacht, *The Flying Cloud.* Chanel didn't swim and found the ocean boring. He also gave her a checkbook linked to his account (possibly he also owned the bank). She returned it after the split without ever having written a single check. Despite the Everest-high society and engorged rushing river of money, in the end it was the same old thing. Chanel may have been a genius who could read both the stylistic and practical needs of an entire gender and fulfill them, but when it came to love, her troubles resembled those of the simplest seamstress in her atelier. Bendor cheated. Bendor lied. Bendor couldn't understand why Chanel didn't want to sell her business and become the third Duchess of Westminster, about which she is said to have said, "Anyone can be a duchess but there is only one Chanel." He cheated some more. Ditto lied. Near the end of the affair, he invited his newest paramour to join him and Chanel aboard *The Flying Cloud.* Chanel, humiliated and furious, ordered his new grilfriend off at the next port. Bendor, duly chastised, gave Chanel either a rope of magnificent pearls or yet another sapphire, which she tossed overboard.

Pierre Reverdy
Unrequited love
1920s, no one agrees on the exact years

Reverdy was a professional, tortured poet and friend of Picasso, Matisse, Louis Aragon, and other surrealists who became rich and famous while he was left behind. He gnashed his teeth with both envy and revulsion and lived only for his work, in complete squalor. André Breton called Reverdy the greatest poet of the age. He would not allow Chanel to do for him what Boy Capel had done for her—namely, underwrite his talent (although he would accept a small, regular stipend). He was married to a beautiful young woman named Henrietta, with whom he moved to a Trappist abbey, where he became a lay brother. Chanel adored his dark moods, his poetic soul, the fact that she couldn't have him. His greatest gift to her was not his love, but his writing advice. Chanel loved a well-turned phrase as much as she did a perfect sleeve. He steered her toward La Rochefoucauld's *Sentences et Maximes* and encouraged her to read a few each evening to get the hang of making a good aphorism. "True generosity means accepting ingratitude," she said. Chanel was always a quick study.

Paul Iribe

Fellow temperamental type, visual artist, and almost-fiancé
1933–1935

Iribe was a basque caricaturist who also worked at one time as a designer for Chanel's nemesis, Paul Poiret. That minx Colette described him as "chubby as a capon."* With Chanel's friend Jean Cocteau, Iribe founded a magazine, *Le Mot.* He spent the 1920s slaving away

---

A castrated rooster, not to be confused with a caper, that green eraser-size bud thing often called for in Italian recipes.

in Hollywood, designing sets for Cecil B. DeMille, and according to Chanel, never forgave her for the fact that she was the toast of Paris during its golden years, while he was stuck in the depressing, sun-bleached no-man's-land of Southern California. He secretly wanted her to lose her money so she would be dependent on him (according to Chanel). He felt patronized when she allowed him to make decisions for her that were of no real consequence (according to Iribe). Stormy arguments ensued. Chanel was fifty and was said by her friends to be in love for the first time (no one knew her during her salad days on the Avenue Gabriel with dashing Capel). Marriage was in the air. Then, on Chanel's tennis court at La Pausa, in early summer 1935, Iribe collapsed and died of heart failure. Chanel was inconsolable, then picked herself up and went on.

Hans Gunther von Dincklage, aka Spatz

Incontrovertible evidence that people behave unexpectedly during wartime

1940–1950

Spatz was a French-speaking, half-English German spy who Chanel may have known before the war. He never wore a Nazi uniform but was presumed to be part of Foreign Minister Joachim von Ribbentrop's team of smooth talkers installed in Paris to improve the reputation of the invaders. Spatz was a genteel lover of fine food, thirteen years Chanel's junior. There was no getting around the fact that by involving herself with Spatz, she was sleeping with the enemy. After the war they moved to Switzerland.

There were other assignations. A fleeting one with Igor Stravinsky and also probably Picasso. But at the end of her life, she claimed that after the death of Boy in 1919 love eluded her. "I lost everything when I lost Capel," she told Paul Morand in her dotage, thus contradicting the conventional wisdom that the only way to get over someone is to get under someone else.

What then is the solution to the merciless throttling of grand passion? The Anna Karenina option is no option at all, if only because there is nothing worse than spending eternity regretting having thrown yourself under a train for some guy. Instead, we might consider the following:

Surviving Passion á la Chanel

Throw Yourself into Your Work.

"Work has always been a kind of drug for me," said Chanel, who was known to rip out and restitch a shoulder twenty-seven times and despised Sundays because her seamstresses had the day off. The contemporary term for this behavior is workaholic, which has such a disparaging, dysfunctional sound. Fellow Frenchman, writer, and Nobel Prize–winner François Mauriac felt work was a source of bliss and called it *opium unique*, a "unique opium."

You can lose yourself in work, just as you can in wallowing in the memories of a doomed love affair. The difference is that rehashing what cannot be changed (What if I'd loved him better? Been more available? Less available? Hadn't paid him back for fronting me the cash to launch my fashion house?) is an enormous waste of time and energy, while channeling all that angst into work may result in the creation of the little black dress. Also, work is reliably available to all of us all of the time, whereas love in all of its permutations is less reliable than a pot-smoking contractor.

Enjoy Being Loved.

Chanel loved men. Better yet, she loved being loved by them. Even though the desertion and death of Capel had left her feeling as if her heart had been wrapped around the axle of a large truck, that didn't prevent her from diving into other, subsequent liaisons that presumably brought her joy. It's possible that once the pressure is off and we either realize we've already loved and lost "the one" or accepted that he's not likely to parachute into our lives anytime soon, or kicked around the idea that maybe all-consuming passion is the stuff of myth and should be put in the same category as the Loch Ness monster, we might find ourselves seeing someone who's just okay and realize that just okay is pretty dang good. About her relationship with the Duke of Westminster, Chanel said, "I loved him, or thought I loved him, which is the same thing." Believing can be feeling.

Buy a Horse.*

Let's return to Balsan for a minute. We hear a lot about how he liked Chanel and was amused by her, but after she flew the breeding farm

---

I wish I could also recommend buying a dog or cat, but for some reason they are less all consuming.

with Capel, there's no mention of his response. That's because regardless of the state of his love life, the horses needed to be worked; rubbed down; groomed with first the hard brush then the soft; fed their hay, their grain, and any special vitamins; given special beet pulp to encourage good digestion; checked for worms, founder, laminitis; then worked, rubbed down, groomed with first the hard brush, then the soft, fed their hay, and so forth and so on, forever and ever, amen. Horses can consume every waking hour of your life, plus they have such pretty eyes. Chanel's friend Winston Churchill famously said, "No hour of life is wasted that is spent in the saddle." The same cannot be said of our loved ones.

Count Your Blessings (No. 1).

It really is better to have loved and lost. Having been flattened by the semitruck of love (this chapter appears a little heavy on the transportation images—forgive me) is one of life's great absorbing personal dramas, and not everyone is privileged to suffer the experience. Some of us go to our graves never having spent six months drunk-Googling, or peering into the windows of our beloved the night of his first date with someone else. . . . Failing to endure such misery is to spend a life never really understanding why people routinely cite Every Rose Has Its Thorn as the greatest hair band ballad of all time.

Count Your Blessings (No. 2).

Chanel railed against her failed love life because it hadn't included the marriage and children she believed would have made her happy and cure her deep and abiding loneliness. It's a cliché of the unhappily married that there's no lonelier place to be than inside an empty marriage, but this never occurred to her.

Marriage, like mountain climbing, isn't for everyone. She, who was so full of air-tight maxims about so many things, entirely missed the fact that she was constitutionally ill equipped to be a dutiful wife. That she would have been required to, if not submit, then compromise, was a concept as foreign to her as, uh, compromise. As for children, Chanel struggled with the demands of dog ownership. She went through an Afghan-owning phase, which consisted of having Joseph the butler parade the dogs through her rooms on their leashes. There was always an awkward moment after their promenade when she was expected to pet them. Chanel had a horror of bad odors, and we can only surmise that doggy breath would be one of them.

But even though Chanel called Freud a joke—and tossed in the rest of soul-searching for good measure—she wasn't completely ignorant of her inner workings. She understood well the central dilemma: "God knows I wanted love . . . but the moment I had to choose between the man I loved and my dresses, I chose the dresses."

In her old age she was a pain in the ass to anyone who would listen to her litany of self-pity. It was sad and exhausting. She was a windup doll of her former self. In her obsession with marriage as a cure-all her solitude—forgetting, as does everyone who puts all her eggs in the basket of matrimony, that divorce is common and widowhood not uncommon—she failed to grasp one of the basics of human relationships. In the words of the normally windy Henry James,

"True happiness, we are told, consists in getting out of one's self; but the point is not only to get out—you must stay out; and to stay out you must have some absorbing errand." Chanel sentimentalized marriage, but maybe all she ever needed was an absorbing errand outside herself.

Anyway, Count Your Blessings (No. 2). One of the great unsung advantages of not having all your dreams come true, especially if you're someone like Chanel, who made every other dream of hers come true, is that there remains something out, there just beyond reach, on which you can blame all your misery. You truly can't always get what you want, and it's a good thing, too. Imagine the horror of attaining everything in life you'd hoped for, yet remaining unhappy? Chanel loved and was loved by many. She possessed a stupendous treasure trove of memories, not to mention a lot of fist-size sapphires.

5

ON EMBRACING THE MOMENT

"Don't spend time beating on a wall,
hoping to transform it into a door."

In the spirit of the title of this chapter, I began my writing day by checking eBay. This was on offer:

> *Chanel jacket. Navy and white tweed. One button front. Single breasted. Inner bottom chain trim. Fringe edging. Button is gunmetal colored with enamel and CC logo center. Shoulder and waist panels are quilted. Fully lined with signature lining. Chest under arms is 17.5", waist 15¾". Total length from shoulder/collar seam all the way down is 23". Brand new, guaranteed authentic, with tags attached.*

And this:

> *Presented is this most recognizable white/black nubby jacket from Chanel. Women's size: 36 and measures approx. Bust 36", Length 20", Sleeve 24". There is signature ivory CC silk lining, weight chain, and black/*

white CC buttons. The fabric content is wool and nylon. This one is a real beauty and in perfect mint condition.

Also:

Limited edition Chanel jacket. Unique cashmere tweed (90% cashmere, 8% cotton). Single breasted. Fully lined with signature black silk lining. Four pockets in front. All with flaps and functioning buttons. Three functioning buttons on each sleeve. All buttons are black with CC logo center. Fringe edges throughout. Signature chain on the bottom inside. Brand new, guaranteed authentic with tags attached. Measurements: chest under arms 17¼", waist 16½", shoulders across back just under 15", total length from shoulder/collar seam all the way down 24".

I'd been "watching" a Chanel jacket ("Authentic CHANEL Tweedy Suit Jacket") for a week. There were a few more hours left to bid, but it appeared my auction gene was on backward. As the clock ticked down, instead of wanting the jacket more ("Unless I put in another bid some stranger is going to nab this jacket and I'll never see it again!"), I found myself wanting it less. ("Fine. I'm low on hangers anyway.")

My basic distrust of eBay was roused when I scrolled through the hyperbole (. . . ultra classy . . . amazing feminine details . . .) and, at the bottom of the page, discovered that the "Authentic CHANEL Tweedy Suit Jacket" was not black and beige, as several pictures suggest, but midnight blue, chocolate brown, and ivory cream. It hardly mattered. I couldn't seem to suppress the niggling feeling that even though the jacket was Chanel (actually Lagerfeld-Chanel, another thing I couldn't quite ignore, but more about that later), it sort of looked like, well, Chico's. *Not* that there's anything wrong with Chico's, aside from an attitude toward bold floral prints that's a little too inclusive and the fact I tried on a jacket there once and was told by my friend that I looked like a nanny. And probably not one of those hip, sexy nannies who steals the heart of a sexy A-list actor from under the nose of his equally sexy wife.

I admire Chico's lack of pretension (they even named a collection after Debbie Phelps, the resolutely mom-looking mom of multi–gold medal Olympic swimmer Michael Phelps), but a Chico's jacket isn't and will never be a Chanel jacket. If I wanted a Chico's jacket, I would just go to the mall and buy one. I wouldn't put myself through all this eBay rigmarole, then shell out a few grand for the privilege. Also, were I to win the tweedy jacket in midnight blue, chocolate brown, and ivory cream tweed, I would feel the urge to announce to friends and strangers alike that this was a *Chanel* jacket, even though it looked like a Chico's jacket, and that felt like a lot of unnecessary wardrobe pressure.

It occurred to me that maybe I didn't want a Lagerfeld-Chanel jacket at all. I remembered reading something Cecil Beaton wrote about designing the costumes for *Coco*, the 1969 Broadway musical starring Katharine Hepburn. He confessed that had he simply copied Chanel's designs, instead of *interpreting* them for the stage, they would have looked like something from a thrift store. Somehow, this got me to thinking that Chanel-Chanel would be preferable after all (please ignore this leap in logic); in being thrift shop–like, it would be easier to come by, not to mention authentic, and possibly cheaper. I decided that if I was going to spring for Chanel, I wanted something made under her rule, not by the pretender to the throne. At the time I didn't realize that this was like saying I wanted a real Picasso, not a tasteful, black-framed museum poster.

I e-mailed one of the more knowledgeable eBay sellers about my new plan and received my answer within the hour.

FROM JUDY @ Madisionavenuecouture.com

Dear K2,

It isn't easy, particularly if you are looking for a specific piece. There are vintage stores all over the country and they sell old Chanel pieces when they get them. You can check out vintage stores on the web and tell them what you are looking for. There are also some vintage books that might direct you to some of the better vintage shops. And, eBay sellers have them every once in a while. The problem is that most of the vintage pieces now available are not 40 or 50 years old, more like 10–25 years old.

Good luck. Judy

This is as good a time as any to attempt to unpack Chanel's atypical genius. The French poet Paul Valéry said there needs to be a word between *talent* and *genius*; whatever that word might be (I am restraining myself from doing the Brangelina word combine), Chanel had it.

Aside from her inborn sense of style, and her unerring ability to see at a glance what was aesthetically incorrect, she was blessed with the ability to inhabit her moment and thus take full advantage of whatever dropped into her lap, while at the same time keeping the near future in her peripheral vision. She was able to recognize luck and squeeze every drop of advantage out of it.

There's no getting around the weird, enchanting fact that for decades she was considered the grandest of grand couturiers even though her skills as a seamstress left a lot to be desired. She learned the basics of sewing at the orphanage in Aubazine, and her Aunt Louise trained her and her sister Antoinette in the more difficult tasks of stitching a perfect curved seam, creating trim from remnants, and making a buttonhole. Still, she was a B- student at best. You can imagine her as a teenager, submitting herself to the lessons every other girl of her station was forced to learn, all the while knowing that she would never involve herself in something requiring this sort of humble discipline, not to mention eyestrain.

In 1915 Coco opened a shop in Biarritz, on the southern coast of France, and employed seamstresses from the region to work for her. One of her first employees was Madame Marie-Louise Deray, who in her old age recalled to Pierre Galante in his affectionate, loose-jointed biography, *Mademoiselle Chanel,* "Mademoiselle Chanel had audacity and incredible nerve, especially since she was more of a milliner and knew very little about dressmaking. But she had innate taste and knew how to explain things to others." In other words, she was good at getting other people to do the real work.

Being a general was one facet of her originality, but she would never have been in the position to employ her troop-commanding skills (in short order Madame Deray had sixty women working beneath her) had she not possessed the basic gift of being able to embrace the moment. Not just the Ram Dassian ability to be here now, but also to seize the day—even when she was not exactly in the position to do so. When Étienne Balsan invited her to come live with him at his horse-breeding farm, she could have demurred, as a more dutiful, high-born girl would have. Or, she could have accessed her infamous determination and thought, "I'm not running off with this clown, I'm sticking to my singing career!" Or, simply, "*Un moment, s'il vous plait!* You're a rich guy with a fabulous place in Paris and you want me to live in the country with you and *breed horses?*"

But no. Some do-it-now, don't-look-back urge sent her straight into the arms of a future she couldn't imagine. She perhaps had less of a choice when Boy Capel came along, sucked into his life by the tractor beam of true love. But even then someone with a more conventional outlook might have pressed her well-connected lover to hook her up with a famous designer, the better to hone her sewing skills and practice her sketching—thought to be a necessary skill for any fashion designer before Chanel. But no. Whatever abilities she possessed at that moment were good enough. She was doing what she could with what she had where she was. Aside from being a so-so-sewer, she also wasn't a draftsman. She couldn't draw a simple hat (I may be exaggerating, but only a little).

She went at designing with her hands, a jar of pins, and a large pair of sharp scissors. She could tell at a glance what was wrong or right with a collar or the drape of a skirt. She relied on master seamstresses to do the rest.

We must stop and smell the irony. The great eccentric visionary Paul Poiret, whose career sank like a stone as Chanel's was on the rise, could both sew and draw. His sketches were so good that before he was hired by designer Jacques Doucet, he made a living selling his drawings to all the major Parisian fashion houses. During the First World War, Poiret was named chief of military tailors, after having designed an overcoat* that saved both materials and labor; after the war ended, his fashion house was near bankruptcy, in part because Chanel's style had trumped his own. As if that weren't enough, she was becoming famous not simply for her uncomplicated clothes with their clean lines and simple construction, but also for their superb craftsmanship, the care and perfection with which everything that left Chanel Modes was made. Poiret possessed the old-fashioned and theatrical notion that gowns and dresses should be "read beautifully from afar." His clothes, up close, were not visions of beauty, beautifully rendered, even though he himself had the talent and skill to produce such garments. Unlike Chanel, whose revolutionary ideas included designing clothes from the inside out, clothes that she, a woman, felt comfortable wearing (imagine!), he designed dresses to be viewed on a comely lady standing perennially across the street.

Perhaps fortunately for Chanel, her awful, desperate childhood

---

He was ordered not to wear his self-designed uniform, which featured a blue silk tie with a naked woman reclining along the length of it.

only served to nurture her penchant for leaping before looking, then figuring out to what use she could put the clouds on the way down. She was never hobbled by the allure of nostalgia, because her past had been so dismal. If she had a knack for living in her own time, it was because there were no good old days, as how could there be? Her Proustian madeleine was a nasty bowl of porridge served at the charity table in an underheated orphanage. She repudiated her past and lied about where she came from; now was always a better place to be than then. This attitude also served to make her seem completely modern.

❈❈❈

Embracing the moment means embracing who you are at the moment. It also demands appreciating who everyone else is in your life. One of Chanel's oft-quoted bons mots on fashion, hippie-like in its inclusiveness, asserts that "Fashion is not just dresses. Fashion is in the sky, in the street, fashion has to do with ideas, the way we live, what is happening." She might have also added, "Fashion depends on who you're dating."

Chanel was an alchemist. She absorbed that which was right in front of her nose, processed it, and then pressed it through her own sensibility. In went the plain, functional duds worn by the grooms and trainers at Royallieu, out came jodhpurs for women.* In went

---

*This, in a time when ladies wore pounds of clothing and little hats in order to ride side-saddle, which, if you've ever ridden a horse with more spunk than a sofa, seems like a posture designed for the maximum opportunity for breaking your neck.

the Duke of Westminster's lavish gifts of emeralds and sapphires, diamonds, and ropes of pearls and out came the notion of costume jewelry—faux-lavish pieces that mimicked the real thing.

Chanel's Muses and
What They Inspired: An Aperçu

Nuns	love of black and white, belief in austerity
Étienne Balsan	riding breeches for women, also tiny knit ties
Boy Capel	blazers, cardigans, the "slipover sweater," belts for the waist
Grand Duke Dmitri	embroidered skirts and dresses; the *roubachka* (long-belted blouses favored by Russian peasant women); tunics (same length, no belt)
Marcel Proust	camellias

Bendor	tweeds; Fair Isle jersey; waist-coats; shirts that called for cufflinks; yachting caps; sailor trousers; berets; neckerchiefs
Pierre Reverdy	snappy maxims

According to Chanel, "Fashion that does not reach the street is not fashion." Somehow this remark was mashed up with her dedication to relieving well-dressed women of their epaulets and furbelows, their jabots and peplums, and everything else that made them feel like a well-appointed piece of parlor furniture (earlier in the century Poiret had launched the trend for making dresses out of upholstery fabric), and the result was the erroneous assumption that her *"genre pauvre"* was inspired by the outfits of clerks and shopgirls.

People missed the point. They equated her simple style with the clothes worn by poor, working women because it was a given that the first thing any woman would do if she came into money would be to trick herself out in a froufrou petticoat and a stack of fake hair.

Perhaps the world was not ready for the cross-dressing implications, but Chanel's style was not lifted from the lower classes (it was permissible to use that descriptor in those days), but from men. People saw her turtlenecks and thought, sailors wear those! Yes, and the only sailors around in those days were men. Men wore blazers, sweaters, trousers, and belted their waists with leather belts, all rendered in tweeds, wools, and the infamous jersey.

Her master stroke was to feminize menswear while at the same time incorporating elements of dress completely at odds with early-twentieth-century notions of elegance. That women's clothes might be chic as well as comfortable was unheard of. Then came Chanel, and for the first time, women could stride down the street in their clothes, hop on a bike, climb into a car—stuff men had been doing all along.

War has traditionally been good for business, but rarely has it been so good for fashion. It's possible that without World War I there would have been no Chanel, which means no Chanel jackets over which to pine, no affordable (relatively speaking) fetching little Chanel quilted bags, and no Chanel No. 19, which some of us prefer to the heavy floral scent of No. 5.

It wasn't simply a matter of luck. It wasn't Chanel sitting in her atelier in Deauville minding her own business, creating casual sportswear for the holiday crowd and then one afternoon picking up the newspaper only to discover Europe was at war.

Chanel and Capel were summering in Deauville when Archduke Franz Ferdinand, heir to the throne of Austria, and his wife were assassinated on June 28. For another month it was better business than usual at Chanel Modes. Fancy ladies with fancier names showed up to purchase Chanel's breezy sportswear. Business was booming in July, thanks to the aforementioned brutal heat wave. At the end of that month, Austria declared war on Serbia (the Archduke had been murdered while on a visit to Sarajevo), who appealed to Russia for help. On the same day, Berlin declared war on Russia—and on France. Somehow Britain was also involved, although perhaps only as a bargaining chip.

The net result for Chanel was that her client base fled (somewhat hastily, as we shall see) back to Paris. Deauville was a ghost town, and Chanel set about closing her shop when Capel, who was out of town and already involved in providing clandestine coal for the Allies, which would make him even richer than he already was, sent her a wire telling her to sit tight. He had friends on the inside, the outside, places high, places low, and everywhere else. He was the possessor of top-secret information. Chanel was notoriously dictatorial with her employees and a stubborn negotiator in most business matters, but she was also good at knowing when to listen. She did nothing.

Chanel waited. Chanel Modes stayed open, even though there were no customers.

The first week of August saw another round of war declaring. Germany officially declared war on France, before invading Belgium. Then Britain declared war on Germany. Three weeks later, the Germans were on the outskirts of Paris. The Western front had been pushed back to the Marne River. The French men joined the army and went to war, while the French women—or the rich ones, anyway—hurried back to Deauville.

They returned in droves, minus two key components: their vast wardrobes and their menfolk. Chanel suspected that women, on their own and with important things to do—they volunteered in hospitals, rolled bandages, visited the wounded, consoled war widows—would naturally gravitate toward a more relaxed, more comfortable style. She suspected that was what they'd wanted all along. Without their men around to disapprove, they cut loose.

The only clothes shop open was Chanel Modes. Determined to maintain their chic, they bought out Chanel's stock of long jersey jackets and slim knit skirts; slipover sweaters, worn belted and cuffed; and small hats they could tuck in a coat pocket.

Chanel was not just apolitical, she was completely deaf to politics (fast-forward to World War II, where her romance with a Nazi sullied her image for good), and in September 1914 all she saw was how to use the turn of events to her advantage. Her impoverished childhood trained her to make do with whatever was at hand, and what was at hand was society in disarray. She said, "A world was dying, while another was being born. I was there, an opportunity came forward and I took it."

It's like the old joke about the two shoe salesmen who set out on a ship to find new places to sell their shoes. They land on an island and are greeted by a huge tribe of friendly, barefoot natives. Salesman One radios back to the front office, "Bad news, boss. Found a new market but they don't wear any shoes." Salesman Two radios back to his front office and says, "Great news, boss! Found a new market and they don't wear any shoes."

Coco Chanel was Salesman Two.

6

ON SUCCESS

"Gentleness doesn't get work done,
unless you happen to be a hen laying eggs."

When Chanel quipped that in the year 1919 she woke up famous, she wasn't joking; she was merely stating a fact. A year earlier, during the depths of World War I, she was rich enough to both pay back Boy Capel and purchase her own chateau near Biarritz. It cost about a million in today's dollars, and she paid cash. (What did she bring to the closing? The quilted bag was years away, and anyway I don't think it would hold that many bills.) This financial tidiness is high on the list of things I admire about Chanel. I don't imagine shady mortgage brokers are a new life-form; she could have easily gotten herself into the early twentieth–century version of a subprime ARM. She could have hoarded the rest of her profits and made impassioned, bogus promises to Capel about when she would return his investment, which I'm sure he'd already written off as the price of being in love.

By the war's end jersey had become the new cashmere and *American Vogue* was singing the praises of Chanel and her sportswear. The humble fabric had turned out to be more versatile than anyone imagined. It was manufactured in various weights and could be pressed into service for suits, skirts, capes and jackets with roomy pockets in which you could thrust your hands. Chanel combined weights and textures. She married jersey and silk. Suede showed up from time to time, and in her winter collections, fur. She expanded her collection, creating ethereal gowns of black Chantilly lace trimmed with jet beading and fluid, long-waisted dresses of dove gray crepe de chine. What would become the classic Chanel palette emerged: beige, taupe, gray, navy blue, and black, sometimes with a splash of red.

The beleaguered genius Paul Poiret had pressed his mannequins into cutting their long, heavy hair as early as 1908. Chanel chopped off her own locks a dozen years later and was credited with creating the bob. She cultivated a tan, and so did everyone else. She was lean, sinewy, and tomboyish (even though, in 1919, she was already thirty-six years old), and every woman who did not want to appear dated slimmed down and sat in the sun without her parasol. The styles of the Belle Époque had died in the war; the pale-cheeked, blown-out pink rose in a bouffant skirt made of some stiff, uncomfortable upholstery fabric was ancient history.

Chanel believed in astrology, as well she should have. She was a Leo, the lion, and thus possessed of passion, strength, determination, self-mastery, and a serious need to show off. Those of us who're born and raised in the woo-woo cities of the West Coast think nothing of factoring in the rest of our birth charts—Chanel's moon was in Pisces, making her intuitive to the point of psychic. It certainly seems as if she could predict the future, at least when it came to waistlines and shoulder widths.

The stars could not possibly have been better aligned. The war with its shortages and rationing provided the perfect environment for spare, easy clothes made from a small amount of inexpensive fabric to flourish. And Capel had not only loved and believed in her enough to bankroll her boutiques (plural), he was also phenomenally well connected, an adviser to French prime minister Georges Clemenceau, as well as part of the Supreme War Council (he was the political secretary of the English delegation), all of which is to say that he had a deep inside track when it came to advising her on when to hold and when to fold and when to open a shop in Biarritz, in southern France, far from the frontlines, which would wind up making her a fortune creating clothes for the rich ladies of neutral Spain.

At the same time, Chanel was becoming better connected. She knew few people when she moved in with Capel on the Avenue Gabriel, and the couple kept a low profile given their sketchy marital state. But in 1917 Chanel was befriended by Misia Sert, infamous Polish patroness of the arts, über-tastemaker, and professional drama queen, described by culture critic Clive James as "the incarnation of that special energy released when talent and privilege meet."

Misia* honed the final rough edges off Chanel, who still bore traces of the timid provincial girl who loved horses and romance novels. She counted among her friends the celebrity artists of the day, including Stéphane Mallarmé, Pierre-Auguste Renoir, Jean Cocteau, Pablo Picasso, and Sergei Diaghilev; soon, they were all Chanel's

---

Like Cher and Madonna, Misia was always known simply as Misia.

friends as well. Their artistic cred rubbed off on Chanel, helping her move into the ranks of the Creative Famous.

As if all this weren't enough, Chanel's atelier on the Rue Cambon sat across from the back entrance to the Ritz. During the hard winters of the war, the Ritz could be counted on to be nicely heated, and fashionable women often stopped in to get out of the cold, after which they would pop over to Chanel Modes for a new frock.

Everything Chanel touched turned to chic. Being in the right place at the right time doesn't begin to cover it. She was the right person of the right gender with the right look and the right sense of style with the right brutal, unforgiving, character-building childhood influencing the right temperament, who met the right *man* with the right temperament with the right kind of belief in her and the right kind of money (loads) during the right cultural and political moment. Even the great tragedy in her life—the loss of Capel—was the right kind of wrong, pushing her to sublimate her grief by working her head off.

I apologize if I've overstated my case, but it would be disingenuous to suggest that all it takes is a little elbow grease, a rabbit's foot, and the love of a good man with a lot of moola to achieve the rarified success that Chanel enjoyed. If you're an aspiring *Project Runway* contestant and have opened this book to find some tips on how you, too, can one day be named the most influential designer in the history of fashion, then I'm afraid I will fail you. There will never be another Chanel.

Which doesn't mean the nature of her stupendous right-place/ right-time success isn't worth investigating. She was the first bona fide celebrity fashion designer, in part because unlike Poiret before her, or even Madeleine Vionnet, who professed a sweet theory of fashion ("When a woman smiles, then her dress should smile too.") but hated publicity and was a virtual recluse, Chanel had a philosophy. Over the years fashion historians who are not fans of Chanel have routinely sneered about her impulse for self-promotion, forgetting that she wasn't simply putting Coco Chanel forward, she was also propagating real ideas.

There was more beneath her clothes than underwear (what did replace the corset, anyway? Granny panties?). Chanel's clothes were cheeky in their simplicity, flawless in their creation, but they were also more than just a belted cardigan, a pleated jersey skirt, a slouchy hat. They had meaning. They had a plot and even a point of view. Everything that left her workroom was meant to be enjoyed first and foremost by the woman inside the garment. She never just tossed collections out there, willy-nilly. She believed in effortlessness, athleticism, and freedom, and everything she made reflected that—except maybe those long ropes of pearls, which you can just imagine getting caught on a doorknob or the arm of a chair.

Chanel worked on every garment that left the Rue Cambon, smoothing, cutting, tucking, pinning, patting, pressing, but she was shrewd enough to make herself unavailable to her customers, the better to shroud herself in a certain mystery. (According to Chanel, "A client seen is a client lost.") She referred to her blue-blooded clientele as her "Little Darlings," but she mistrusted their loyalty. They were never given the chance to get close enough to her to say, "*Zut alors,* did you see the bags under Mademoiselle's eyes?"

Out in the world, at Maxim's, and at parties held by the cream of the aristocracy, Chanel was her own best model—she never wore a stitch that didn't come from her own workrooms—but she also got the word out by giving away her latest gowns to dark-haired, dark-eyed It girls who resembled her, and who made a career of their social lives. She put her friend, English society girl Vera Bate, on permanent retainer; Bate wore only Chanel and when pressed, faux-reluctantly revealed the name of her couturiere.

Chanel kept a careful eye on her growing fame, while at the same time shrugging it off. She liked to claim sole responsibility for creating not just the modern woman's wardrobe, but the entire woman herself, one who strode down the road in her short swingy skirts, smoking, taking lovers, listening to jazz (and tanning, of course), while at the same time demurring that she was nothing more than a simple tradeswoman, a dressmaker, no different from a candlestick maker. She was shameless when it came to taking credit for innovations that belonged to someone else, but if anyone objected, they were never able to make their objections stick.

She adored luxury, but always showed up in the same simple black or navy blue suit. The moment she had two francs to rub together, she purchased a Rolls Royce and hired a driver. She furnished her rooms with fine Louis XIV furniture covered not in jersey, *mais non!*, but in sand-colored satin of the finest quality, and rare Coromandel screens. She hired Maurice Sachs, a struggling writer, to create a library of first editions of everything she should read.

At the same time, Chanel drove herself with the desperate

attitude of someone waiting for her luck to turn. She took nothing for granted. Though her laurels were piling up like a blizzard in Barrow, she refused to rest on them. She rarely rested at all.

There's an old Hollywood adage about what it takes to make it. Listed in ascending order of importance:

3. Have some talent.
2. Know the right people.
1. Be fun to be with.

The engine that drove Chanel's life was work, perfectionism, and a determination to avoid having to rely on anyone—not exactly the carefree traits of a party girl. Without knowing it she shared with world-class mountaineers (another driven, obsessive bunch) the idea that you don't have to have fun to have fun. Had Chanel not allowed herself to be taken under the large, eccentric wing of Misia, she would have no doubt struggled with items 2 and 1, and perhaps wound up with a career that more closely resembled, well, I don't know. Chances are we never would have heard of her. Or there would have still been a listing under *Chanel, Coco* in the fashion history books, but she never would have had a show at the Metropolitan Museum of Art, nor a 215-foot-tall, 10-story flagship store in the swanky Ginza neighborhood of Tokyo, nor whatever that thing was recently where of-the-moment architect Zaha Hadid designed a huge Chanel purse (was it a purse, or did it just contain works of art that paid tribute to the purse?) and stuck it in Central Park.

Misia lubricated Chanel's entry into society, pure and simple. When Chanel met Misia, her bread-and-butter clients numbered two hundred–plus wealthy society ladies, but they weren't rock stars, while the chi-chi Montparnasse bohos whom Misia tirelessly promoted, were. If she could, I'm sure Chanel would rise up from her grave and strangle me with her sinewy artisan hands, but without Misia, she would never have been ". . . the living symbol of every luxury and extravagance of the period."[*]

Maria "Misia" Sophie Olga Godebska Natanson Edwards Sert—I think I've managed to get all the husbands in there—was a Polish piano prodigy who gave all that[**] up to marry Thadée Natanson, founder of the avant-garde literary review *La Revue Blanche*, at which point she began her career as muse/patroness of the arts. You can see her likeness captured in the works of Toulouse-Lautrec, Edouard Vuillard, Pierre Bonnard, Félix Vallotton, and Renoir. She was pretty, but not that pretty—leaving us to believe that either Misia was really good at sitting still, or possessed a snake-charmers magic. Her mystique captured the imagination of the great Pierre-Auguste Renoir, whose heart she broke by refusing to allow him to paint her breasts. (She also broke the heart of other painters, who made her gifts of their finest works, only to see her cut

Described thus by poet Georges Auriac.
**Seriousness, long hours of practice, possible penury.*

the canvases to fit the size of a wall in need of decoration. Still, they never held it against her.)

Parisian society between the wars was as small as it was famous. Everyone knew everyone else, and mostly it was due to the guiding hand of Misia, who was, depending on whom you talked to, either a master at crafting connection and inspiring artists to great heights (according to one admirer she "aroused the genius in people") or else a dangerous and cruel manipulator with too much time on her hands.

Chanel and Misia met at a dinner party at the home of actress Cécile Sorel, known for her portrayal of Célimène in Molière's *The Misanthrope* and for having leopard-skin window coverings in her apartment on the Quai Voltaire. Chanel was alone—Capel was off on coal business or diplomatic business or lady-seducing business— and Misia had just returned from Italy where, along with Picasso and Cocteau, she'd been trying to raise money for the impoverished Ballets Russes. Misia introduced herself to Chanel, complimenting her fur-trimmed red velvet coat, which Chanel then shrugged off and arranged around Misia's shoulders, an example of her infamously eccentric generosity (not to mention brilliant business acumen—for the famous Misia to be seen around town in Chanel's coat would be tremendous free advertising).

Misia developed an immediate girl crush on Chanel and visited her at her shop on the Rue Cambon, which at the time still sold mostly hats but also jackets and sweaters. Chanel was still simply a woman "in trade" and hadn't yet been accepted by society. Mostly she and Capel spent their time working. Like some post–Gilded Age Bill and

Hill, they were focused that grim winter on advancing their careers. Bad weather once again worked in Chanel's favor. Record-breaking cold pushed up the price of coal to three hundred francs (remember Capel's company was France's major supplier) and caused Chanel's fur-trimmed jersey coats and jackets to fly out of her shop.

Misia and her soon-to-be-husband, Catalan muralist and bon vivant José María Sert, saw Chanel and Capel socially (Sert couldn't understand Misia's mania for Chanel, whom he found shy and somewhat ordinary), and the friendship between the two women seemed like your usual chummy get-together with-our-respective-menfolk gatherings. Misia was eleven years older than Chanel, yet she had a nose for the modern. Misia invited them to the premiere of Diaghilev's modern cubist ballet *Parade*. Erik Satie wrote the scandalous music—which included honking car horns and the clacking of typewriter keys—Cocteau wrote the book, and Picasso wrote the music. The program notes were written by Guillaume Apollinaire, who coined the word *surrealism* (*une sorte de surrealisme*). Misia wore a tiara. At the after party she introduced Chanel to Cocteau, who liked to dance on the table. She pointed out Proust. Shy Chanel was the lady-in-waiting.

Given who she became, it's hard to imagine that for a few years Coco Chanel was the Friend of the Prom Queen. But in 1924 Misia ruled and Chanel watched while her friend held court. Chanel had never heard of the artists Misia called friends: Cocteau and his boyfriend, the young novelist Raymond Radiguet; the gentlemen of the Ballet Russes; the impresario Diaghilev; composer Igor Stravinsky; and principal dancer Serge Lifar, who would become one of Chanel's friends 'til the end.

In these early years, waiting and watching was Chanel's default setting. She may or may not have been as shy as she always claimed to be, but she learned most of what she knew by noticing stuff and keeping her mouth shut. Eventually the tiara would be passed to Chanel (figuratively speaking; Chanel would never wear anything so obvious), and people like Cocteau would compete in the Gushing and Vaguely Illogical Proclamation Sweepstakes with such remarks as, "No history of French literature would be complete without citing the name of Coco Chanel," but those days were still ahead.

Misia was lavish with both her favors and her loyalty. Count and Countess Étienne de Beaumont held a costume ball, and even though Chanel was hired to design their costumes, she wasn't invited. Said Misia, "No doubt the Count de Beaumont had acted instinctively in sending an invitation to me only. But Mademoiselle Chanel was *my* friend. I was profoundly offended by her exclusion." Misia stayed home.*

In many ways the complicated, passionate friendship resembled that of BFFs the world over. Misia introduced Chanel to the world of art, then was steamed when she took advantage of her acceptance

---

In less than two years time, the de Beaumonts would beg Chanel to attend their parties, and in 1924 Chanel would hire Étienne de Beaumont to design jewelry for the House of Chanel.

by the cool crowd and slipped Diaghilev a check so that he could mount a revival of Stravinsky's *The Rite of Spring*. Chanel could be downright bitchy; she once said being around Misia made her feel intelligent—then turned around and hired her friend to design costume jewelry after Misia, heartbroken and down on her luck, was forced to divorce the philandering Sert.

It was a connection forged at a time before Chanel's fame made it difficult for her to sustain a genuine friendship. By the end of the 1920s, she was Mademoiselle Chanel. In a breathtakingly short amount of time, she had managed to create a fabulous, chic, rich, and famous creature to whom she was also hostage; she was convinced that people who might become her friends were only after her money. She also felt the strange urge to expound, to deliver her thoughts in the maxims that her lover, the unsung poet Pierre Reverdy, helped her craft. People were impressed by her wit and intelligence and charmed by her presence, but this didn't invite intimacy.

French women are notorious for their disinterest in having girl-friends. They love men, but women are competition and thus not to be trusted. In her old age Chanel kvetched to anyone who would listen about how lonely she was; it never seemed to occur to her that a friend—not an acolyte nor a butler nor yet another writer she would hire then fire to write her memoirs, but a good old-fashioned best friend—might have eased her suffering.

The greatest success of Chanel's life was not the creation of the little black dress (which Chanelore says she whipped out in ninety minutes, give or take, on a slow afternoon), the invention of costume jewelry, or the smart bouclé suit embraced in the 1960s by Jackie Kennedy.

You're probably ahead of me, because as you turned the page, you raised your arm, the crook of your comely elbow passed within smelling range, and you got a whiff of *rose du mai* or jasmine, maybe some vetiver. If you only recently applied your Chanel No. 5, you might smell the nose-tingling top notes, the white floral-smelling but entirely artificial aldehyde molecules that set Chanel No. 5 apart from every other perfume when it was introduced in 1920, 1921, 1922, or 1923 (depending on which version of Chanelore is accurate).

Five, as they call it in the perfume trade, is still the world's most popular perfume; the company estimates that somewhere in the world a bottle is sold every fifty-five seconds. How long it's been selling at this rate is unknown. We do know that during World War ll, even after Chanel had closed her house, bottles of No. 5 were leaving the boutique in record numbers, purchased first by German soldiers and then the liberation officers—presents for their various females back home.

It's no wonder Chanel's esteemed and thorough biographers haven't been able to agree on the year No. 5 took society by storm; no one can quite agree on the origins of No. 5 either. That's how Mademoiselle Misinformation would want it. The perfume world traffics in mystery (one review of Chandler Burr's *The Perfect Scent: A Year Inside the Perfume Industry in Paris and New York* describes the industry as "insular, glamorous, strange, paranoid, idiosyncratic, irrational, and lucrative"), and the story surrounding Chanel's signature scent would always be inscrutable, yet totally charming, as befits an iconic perfume.

Chanel wasn't the first couturier to create her own perfume, and as usual, when she wasn't the first to do something, she completely revolutionized the concept to such a degree that she could then *claim* to be first. She changed the rules, then congratulated herself for being the only person chic enough to follow them.

Before No. 5, perfumes relied on a single floral scent, which smelled heavy, plodding, and as if it was created not to underscore a woman's allure but to cover up some serious B.O. They had ridiculous, over-the-top names like Hearts Aflame (I'm translating into English for full effect), or desperately melodramatic names like Le Sang Francais* or Le Fruit Defendu**—and came in ultrafancy bottles that could be confused with holy relics. In other words the whole business was antithetical to Chanel's modern sensibility.

Apparently, Chanel was indifferent to the idea of launching a perfume until:

1. Her then-lover, Grand Duke Dmitri Pavlovich, introduced her to his pal Ernest Beaux, another Russian émigré who'd fled the Russian Revolution. Beaux's father had been per-

---

French Blood. Eeew.
**The Forbidden Fruit, which has to be the only name in the world that sounds better in English than it does in French.*

fumer to the Czar, and at the time Beaux met Chanel, he was working for Coty. Pavlovich, who loved luxury as much as Chanel did, said she could not have a world-class fashion house without a world-class perfume to go with it.

2. In the summer of 1923, Chanel and her new acquaintance Colette went antiques hunting in the south of France in Chanel's Rolls Royce. Colette had divorced her second husband and was living with Maurice Goudeket in a small village not far from Roquebrune. Given Chanel's devotion to her work, it's hard to imagine her poking around Provençe with the era's most infamous voluptuary, oohing and aahing over vintage knife sharpeners or quaintly rusted garden furniture. At any rate, in their travels Chanel and Colette stumbled upon the small village of Grasse and toured the Fragonard perfume factory, and Chanel conceived a need to have her own perfume. She contacted a random local perfumer—Ernest Beaux—who discovered she owned a powerful and discerning sense of smell. "Yes," Chanel confessed, "when someone offers me a flower, I can smell the hands that picked them."

3. One of Misia's many contacts came to her with a document that was allegedly found among the papers of the deceased Empress Eugénie, wife of Napoleon III. Called "The Secret of the Medicis," it detailed a here-

tofore top-secret formula for a special toilet water used by the Medici queens (as well as some random, high-class courtesans) that guaranteed "ravishing skin and the complexion of a young girl" and "permanent, inde-structible youth." Misia thought the whole thing was hilarious—magical toilet water, indeed—but it did give her an idea. She ordered a car around and went straight to Chanel, to whom she proposed the idea of producing a world-famous eau de toilette based on "The Secret of the Medicis." The whole saga cracked Chanel up as well, but together the two friends set about experi-menting with packaging, including a square bottle that looked as though it was straight from the apothecary and not the perfumers. Misia, according to her account, seriously encouraged her friend to "really go in for per-fumes." And so she did.

In any case, Beaux and Chanel were a match made in olfactory heaven. Chanel haunted Beaux's lab, sniffing and sniffing until another woman would have become dizzy with nausea. Being blessed with a discerning nose is a lot like being born with perfect pitch. Chanel's nose, like her taste, was flawless. She wanted her perfume to smell not like roses or irises or jasmine, but like itself. She listened when Beaux suggested using synthetic molecules, grasped the nuances of using something artificial not only to mimic a real scent, but to "fix" it, so that it wouldn't fade. Conceptually she liked the idea of a perfume being a constructed thing, like a beautifully designed dress. As for the name, it was either the fifth formula Beaux had offered for her approval, her lucky number, or a number she selected at random just to make everyone wonder. Which they have to this very day.

7

ON CULTIVATING ARCH RIVALS

"The only way not to hate azaleas is to cut them."

I can't leave the charming story of the birth of No. 5 without mentioning how Chanel spread the word that she had a new perfume. Her marketing method was perhaps more genuinely Chanelian than the fragrance itself, which has been described in the *New York Times* as "a bank of white-hot searchlights washing the powdered stars at a movie premiere in Cannes on a dry summer night," a collection of words that don't shout Coco Chanel, so much as they do Strained Metaphor.

Indeed, these days, almost every luxury fragrance could be described as being hot, in part because almost every luxury fragrance is created on the strength of a brief submitted to one of a handful of fragrance manufacturers. Whether the brief arrives from, say, LVHM (Louis Vuitton, Givenchy, Marc Jacobs, Fendi, Parfums Christian Dior, Guerlain, Benefit Cosmetics) or Richemont (Cartier, Van Cleef & Arpels, Chloé), multinational corporations in possession of all those brands that favor full-page color ads shilling fine leather handbags with the aid of androgynous Russian models pretending to be lesbians, it usually always boils down to the same thing: "We want something Hot! Sexy! Young! But not too young! Not feloniously young! Did we mention Hot? And of course, made from inexpensive ingredients that we sell for eight hundred times what it costs to manufacture! We want a white-hot searchlight!"*

From the time Chanel sold her first straw boater to her first Lady-Who-Lunches, she was less than enamored of the upper crust. Her Little Darlings were spoiled, demanding, silly, and, more to the point, failed to pay their bills on time. Chanel couldn't give a fig about biting the well-cared-for hands that fed her. One thing she'd learned early on about dealing with the rich (whom she never counted herself among, since every sou she had she made herself, with nothing more than her "artisan's hands") was that as much as they enjoyed overpaying for anything fashionable, they really enjoyed thinking they had a hand in discovering the chic new thing. Thus Chanel didn't simply drop Colette and her antique Provençal serving platters off at her idyllic neighboring village and speed back to Paris, where she sent out a press release announcing the creation of Chanel No. 5, then wait for her customers to stampede in and buy a bottle.

Instead, Chanel returned with a few unlabeled vials that she gave only to her best clients. Like so many other things, Chanel was ahead of the free-giveaway-with-purchase curve. Only instead of giving her

---

It perhaps goes without saying that this is not true of Parfums Chanel, which still does things the old-fashioned way, employing its own in-house perfumers who create the sister scents of No. 5 in a lab at Chanel world headquarters in Neuilly.

favorite Little Darlings tubes of unpopular lipstick colors and tiny bottles of the toner that no one ever uses, she tucked in a sample of No. 5. And the Little Darlings returned, wanting to know where they could buy some of her fabulous white-hot searchlight-like gift fragrance. She told them she didn't make perfume, this was just a little something for her favorite, most chic and wonderful customers, something she picked up on impulse when she was poking around the sleepy medieval streets of Grasse, in the exotic south. The Little Darlings said, "But you must start manufacturing some of this!" To which Chanel said, "Oh no, I couldn't possibly."

The Little Darlings said, "But you MUST! It's fantastic."

Chanel said, "Oh dear, you really like it?"

The Little Darlings said, "We must have it! When can we buy it?"

At the same time, Chanel was pestering Beaux to step up production.

What happened next was catastrophic, if only in principle. Knowing that the wife of a civil servant could not afford one of her dresses, but could easily splurge for a small bottle of scent (the same doctrine rules the sale of luxury brands today), Chanel called Théophile Bader, owner of Galeries Lafayette. We must pause for a moment to enjoy what must have been on Chanel's part a feeling of pure triumph, as she reintroduced herself to the guy who sold her all those cheap straw boaters a mere half-decade earlier. It was conquering hero time. She was now Chanel, lifestyle star of the temerarious Twenties, returning to see whether Bader would like to stock her new perfume. He demurred, saying he would love to, of course, but he would need more of the stuff than Beaux, who was a nose and not a manufacturer, could possibly produce.

Bader said he knew a pair of brothers who had a factory. It may have sounded to Chanel's ears as it sounds here, benign and nonthreatening, a prelude to a Two Guys Went Into a Bar joke; she figured she would be able to manipulate these brothers with a few well-placed witticisms murmured in her low smoker's voice. But the Wertheimers, Pierre and Paul, owned Les Parfumeries Bourjois, France's largest fragrance company. They were to business what she was to fashion. In Pierre—dapper, brilliant, a womanizer with a taste for fine art and fine thoroughbreds—she had met her match.

They met at Longchamp. The rapport was instant. She was swept away, and rightly so, for Pierre was most interested in that which she found most interesting about herself, the growing empire that was Chanel. Of course Monsieur Wertheimer was delighted to manufacture and distribute Chanel No. 5 as long as Mademoiselle was willing to incorporate.

Marry in haste, repent in leisure. The mess and misunderstandings began almost immediately. Chanel took joy in proclaiming that what she did should never be mistaken for art; that she knew artists and she was no artist, merely an artisan, a tradeswoman, a simple dressmaker. It was a disingenuous ploy, yet more proof that the woman was coy to a nearly perverse degree, that like her costume jewelry, in which she mixed rare gems and colored glass, she simply liked to mess with people.

But when you read about the shockingly lousy deal she made with Pierre, it becomes clear that a lot of the time she really was completely out of her league. She had business sense, but no business education. She treated Pierre like she might a suitor, a manservant, or even one of her Little Darlings. She behaved as if his suggestion to incorporate were beneath contempt, even though she was amenable to the idea. She tossed her business card in his direction and said she'd be happy with 10 percent, but that otherwise she really didn't want to be bothered, didn't want to "have to answer to anyone"—a terrific show of confidence if you were vying for the Championship Pot–Limit Hold'em at the World Series of Poker, but not the best way to approach what would be a lifelong business partnership.

She settled for the measly 10 percent to assure Pierre would keep his manicured paws off her fashion house, which he never showed an interest in anyway. Even Bader insisted on 20 percent. (It's arguably the most well-compensated introduction in history; in 1971 Chanel's personal worth was fifteen million—seventy-six million in today's dollars, give or take—almost all of which came from her cut of the profits from Parfums Chanel.)

At any rate, Chanel was hosed. Chanel No. 5 would become the best-selling perfume in history. During World War II American GIs would buy bottles by the dozens for the ladies back home (so giddy were they to get their hands on it, they never stopped to think that it would be mildly creepy to smell the same scent on their moms as on their girlfriends). Marilyn Monroe would famously purr that it was the only thing she wore to bed, and Andy Warhol would elevate it to icon status by giving it the Campbell Soup silkscreen treatment. And even though Chanel Parfums have introduced other scents—including No. 19, my personal favorite—nothing has ever rivaled No. 5.

In many ways Pierre Wertheimer was Chanel's true husband. They enjoyed a few years of bliss (in the early 1930s she further compounded her problems by signing over her power of attorney to him. Why, Coco, why?), then spent the next several decades fighting for custody of the child.

Legal maneuverings are rarely interesting, and the endless haggling over Chanel's rights with regard to No. 5 is no different. It went on and on and *on,* and she was never able to secure more than the original 10 percent profit she'd agreed to in 1924. The index of Pierre Galante's biography *Mademoiselle Chanel* tells the story.

Wertheimer, Paul 146
> *problems with Chanel, 181, 182, 183–184, 191, 192, 193*
Wertheimer, Pierre
> *influence on Chanel, 143*
> *partnership with Chanel, 143, 147*
> *problems with Chanel, 149, 150, 181, 182, 183–184, 191, 192, 193*

By 1928, Parfums Chanel had to hire a lawyer full-time just to deal with Chanel and her lawsuits.

Finally, after a good fifteen years of wrangling, including one boffo five-year court battle, Chanel did something shocking and to many, unforgivable, forgetting that however beautiful her dresses were, however magnificent her sense of style, however charming her dark-haired, small-boned, narrow-hipped little person, she was at heart not only a shrewd peasant, a canny Chanel from the Auvergne or wherever, she was also a gladiator—a distinction I feel must be made. I know it has meaning in France, but for the rest of us, when we think of French provincials, they're all sort of lovable, feisty lavender soap-scented *Toujours Provence* characters. But Chanel's childhood experience of deprivation, death, loss, and searing disappointment created in her a take-no-prisoners attitude that those of us from nice middle-class backgrounds can't possibly imagine.

Once World War II was in full swing, the Germans started confiscating Jewish-owned businesses. The Wertheimers were Jewish, but Chanel was not. She thought she could leverage this Nazi loophole to her advantage, get out of her lousy binding agreement with Pierre, and reclaim what was rightfully hers—the perfume that she and Beaux had created nearly twenty years earlier. But the Wertheimers were way ahead of her. They'd already made the certifiably French Félix Amiot, an airplane propeller manufacturer who was willing to be their Aryan beard, co-owner of Parfums Chanel. They'd even managed to find a German bureaucrat who would declare in another flurry of legal paperwork that all contacts and agreements made between Parfums Chanel and Mademoiselle Chanel were still binding, in perpetuity.

You would think this would be the end of it. But after the war ended the Wertheimers regained control of their company, and the lawsuits started back up as if nothing had happened.

Despite this epic wrangling, Chanel liked Pierre. Many times over the course of the years she would damn him to hell, then call him *mon cher* Pierre, sometimes within the same phone call. It was a *folie à deux,* literally "madness for two." Since the French have a chic, ready-made phrase for such a thing, they are obviously very good at it. The French also gave us the concept of *jolie laide*, "beautiful ugly." Apply this easy embrace of opposites to the sphere of relationships and you get people who are good at loving people they hate, hating people they love, and killing everyone in between with kindness or cruelty, sometimes both, in the span of time it takes to do the double-cheek air kiss.

As an American, and thus someone genetically hardwired to struggle with ambiguity in relationships—I love my lover, daughter, friends; like a lot of my acquaintances, colleagues, neighbors, and moms of my daughter's friends; dislike a lot of those same people (including a few exes); and hate my enemies (or would, if I had the energy)—I marvel at Chanel's habit of torturing those she loved. Even more incredible still, it didn't seem to make people feel any less devoted to her.

If Misia was Chanel's woman friend, Cocteau was her gay friend. Cocteau, as any dreamy Francophile liberal arts major can tell you, was the whirling poetic center of that over-romanticized artistic vortex centered in Montparnasse: Paris in the 1920s. Cocteau was the hyphenate's hyphenate, a poet-painter-novelist-playwright-filmmaker, and of course, boxing manager.*

In the realm of karmic debt, Chanel owes Cocteau (maybe that's why she disparaged him). Before Cocteau, the Chanel aesthetic may have been everywhere—the war was over and women were free, free, free at last; they lopped off their hair, wore cardigans and belts, and looked like paperboys—but Chanel herself was still the shy pilot fish attached to the side of the gilded pelagic that was Misia Sert. And at Chanel Modes, aside from a few actresses and It girls—the 1920s' equivalent of young, red carpet B-listers most famous for marrying the much-tattooed guitarists of alt-rock bands—Chanel's clientele consisted of the carriage trade. Who else could afford her astronomical prices? And then as now, the carriage trade was, well, stodgy. In the famous Mac vs. PC computer commercials they're PC, only in better suits.

But becoming friends with Cocteau and his avant-garde artist pals conferred upon Chanel a high-gloss sheen of über stylishness (white-hot searchlights!) that was eclipsed for a decade or so mid-twentieth century, but has never really deserted her. After she fell in with Cocteau, not only were her clothes all the rage, *she* was all the rage, living at the red-hot center of Parisian artistic life, partying late

Cocteau discovered a drug-addicted boozehound and former prizefighter named Panama Al Brown in a Paris nightclub and decided to launch Brown in a comeback attempt. Why he did this is anyone's guess—some connection between verse and the poetry of boxing? The basic artistic impulse to procrastinate? Weirder still, Cocteau's efforts were underwritten by Chanel, who sent Brown to rehab (she loved sending people to rehab); the tale ended happily with Brown regaining his European title.

into the night at Le Boeuf sur le Toit (The Ox on the Roof) with a nexus of poets, painters, musicians, theater types, art dealers, and, yes, the fringe of the carriage trade, the really rich folks who had a taste for the wild side.

Thus, at the intersection of Art and Commerce sat Chic, in the person of Coco Chanel. Talk about your cross-branding! Without too much trouble Cocteau conned her into designing the costumes for his production of *Antigone* (it doesn't get more artistically high-falutin' than that). Characteristically, Chanel defied conventional wisdom and stuck the actors in heavy Scotch woolens, which would have given Sophocles' Greeks heatstroke, not to mention an itchy rash. The press praised her ensembles as being accurate and authentic. She went on to make a mini-career of costume design, stepping up to the plate once again for both *Le Train Bleu* and *Orphée*.

Meanwhile, Chanel helped with Cocteau's bills, specifically the steep cost of rehab. Known quaintly as "the cure," everything back then was more romantic, even drug addiction, specifically opium drug addiction. At the risk of revealing my total naiveté regarding such matters—do they even have such a thing anymore? Isn't opium the puffy-shirt, poetry-writing great-grandpa of heroin?

Anyway, Cocteau began smoking the stuff in earnest after the death of his lover, the literary prodigy Raymond Radiguet. Nicknamed *Monsieur Bébé*, Mister Baby, by a gang of pals that included Juan Gris, Picasso, Ernest Hemingway, and Chanel, Radiguet published his first novel, *The Devil in the Flesh,* when he was twenty (he'd been writing since he was fifteen). While revising his second novel, he came down with a fever. A doctor diagnosed pneumonia, but Chanel smelled a misdiagnosis and sent around her own MD, who identified Radiguet's typhoid, which was too advanced to treat. When the boy died, Chanel organized his funeral, which was, of course, devastatingly simple, beautiful, and expensive: The church was full of nothing but white flowers, with the exception of a few red roses strewn on Radiguet's white coffin.

Chanel loved Cocteau's high energy, his lavish creativity, and his ability to get himself into trouble, from which she would then be forced to rescue him. In 1928, when he was on the verge of entering another Chanel-underwritten attempt at the cure, he decided he needed one last smoke.

Then as now, drug dealers tended toward the sketchy, and when Cocteau met his connection at some low-life café, he was held hostage (or so the apocryphal story goes). Somehow he was able to get word to Chanel that he'd been kidnapped (how?), and Chanel, afraid to call the police because she'd be forced to reveal Cocteau's illegal habit, staged a daring rescue. Let's take a moment to imagine Chanel to the rescue, racing down a narrow, cobblestone French street in her navy blue jersey suit, ropes of pearls a-swingin', her straw boater flying off her head. That's not what happened, of course, but what did happen is just as bizarre. She put in a call to Marcel Thil, the French middle-weight boxing champion (whom she knew through Cocteau's boxing connections) and inquired whether he'd be available for a little hostage rescue. He was thrilled to be of service, and when he showed up at the low-life cafe, Cocteau was released without a fight.

In the end, though, Cocteau wound up getting on Chanel's nerves. On behalf of her beloved Pierre Reverdy, she resented Cocteau for his fame, in particular all the huzzahs over what she felt was his shallow, crowd-pleasing poetry.

Delivering a devastating bon mot was not just all the rage in the cafe society of 1920s Parisian culture, it was also a sport, in which Chanel effortlessly excelled. Sometimes, if she felt like making Cocteau cry, she would tell him he wasn't a real poet. Sometimes she referred to him as an amusing little insect. Once, in an interview in an American magazine, she called him ". . . a snobbish little pederast who did nothing all his life but steal from people." Ouch.

Still, when Cocteau was elected to the Académie Française in 1955, Chanel donated the largest gem for his sword. Yes, sword. France is a nation that so reveres the power of their greatest minds that part of the honor of being inducted into the academy is receiving your own sword, suitable for . . . well, who knows what they do with it. After his appointment is announced, friends of the honoree make secret donations on his behalf at the esteemed Arthus-Bertrand ("Engravers, Embroiderers, and Jewelers since 1803"); when he arrives to choose his weapon, he finds out in short order how beloved he really is. It can be a humiliating moment. But Chanel made sure her amusing little insect was provided for, in the form of a nice big rock for the hilt.

Cocteau said of his friend, "Her spectacular liaisons, her rages, her nastiness, her fabulous jewels, her creations, her whims, her excesses, her kindness as well as her humor and generosity, all these were part of her unique, endearing, attractive, excessive, and very human personality. . . . She looks at you tenderly, then nods her head and you're condemned to death."

Chanel's relationships with Pierre Wertheimer and Cocteau may have been rivalrous, but a part of Chanel loved them. We must never forget that once she started making money, she bred her own thoroughbreds and loved nothing more than a good horse race (complete with jockeys whipping not their mounts down the homestretch, but each other). Technically, both men were her *frenemies*, a good and new American word that conveys, to the best of our unsophisticated ability, how you can cherish a friend who is also an enemy.

Which brings us to Chanel's true archrival, the villain in hot pink, Elsa Schiaparelli. Throughout the space launch that was Chanel's career (up, up, up, and UP!), she had rivals: Poiret, who held Chanel personally responsible for turning women into emaciated little telegraph clerks, and Jean Patou, who was so was jealous of Chanel, he'd snap up the new issue of *Vogue* the moment it appeared at the corner tabac and obsessively tally up how many pages were devoted to him and how many to her (what he did with this figure aside from torture himself to death is unknown). But no one fried Chanel's bacon like Schiap, aka The Italian.

A disclaimer: I am a fan of hot pink, Schiap's signature color. I also like that red and white silk organza dress with the red lobster on the front from her summer 1937 collection. The lobster was designed by Salvador Dali* and the dress made famous when it was modeled by Wallis Simpson, the future Mrs. Duke of Windsor, in *American Vogue*. Schiap lost me with the shoe-hat, which, if you can picture it, was worn with the black felt "toe" pointing forward in the manner of a driving cap, and the high heel pointing heavenward in the manner of a radio antenna. It was said to be inspired by Man Ray, who liked to wear his wife's shoes on his head.

The Italian's clothes were witty. In the same way Chanel made her name by feminizing menswear, Schiap made hers by showing that clothes could be stylish and playful, even funny. The enigmatic Basque fashion innovator Cristóbal Balenciaga said, "Coco had very little taste, but it was good. Schiap, on the other hand, had lots of it, but it was bad." The upshot, as far as we moderns are concerned is this: If sloppy sweatpants are the endgame of the Chanel philosophy of fashion, then lurid holiday sweaters must be blamed on Schiap.

Anyway, as a self-appointed apologist for Coco Chanel, I am both obligated and happy to point out that she was horrified by The Italian's shenanigans. She firmly believed that women should be beautiful, not eccentric.

There must have been a number of things about Schiap that put Chanel's nose out of joint. First, if not foremost, the woman was born in a *palace*, the Palazzo Corsini, in Rome, where her father, an Italian intellectual, was paid handsomely to run the palatial library. Her family included the famed astronomer Giovanni Schiaparelli, who

---

*Dali was denied permission to throw mayonnaise at the mannequin for a full sense-o-round surreal experience.

named the seas and continents of Mars and shared his love, of the stars with his little niece, Elsa, on whose wee cheek he identified a pattern of tiny moles whose pattern resembled the Big Dipper. (If you listen carefully you can hear the sound of Chanel snorting with derision from beyond the grave.) Schiap went on to study philosophy in a desultory fashion at the University of Rome, before publishing an overheated collection of poetry that featured the perennial teen combo platter of sex and mysticism, which prompted her dad to stick her in a convent and then, when she went on a hunger strike, hurry to collect her.

All this male attention, all this fatherly love, all this banishing and rescuing and fond freckle naming! Compare and contrast, please, with Chanel's illegitimate birth in the poorhouse, the death of her mother, the abandonment of her father, the orphanage. How it must have irked her. No one really knows how much she actually knew about her rival, but we can assume that like most crafty people who know more than they let on, she was well aware of their differences.

Chanel was the undisputed fashion queen of the 1920s, but by the 1930s Schiap was threatening to dethrone her. At the turn of the decade, Chanel was showing clothes that were definitely more girly than the feminized menswear she'd had such success with after the war. Low-waisted, bust-denying sheaths were out; form-fitting dresses with bloused bodices, belted waists, and flowing skirts were in. Chanel still showed her suits, but with frilly cuffs and cravat bows. She was on a serious black-and-white kick, and if she sprang for an accent color, it was usually green or brown, or that festive smidge of red. Her evening wear was positively over-the-top by her austere standards—she got into sequins, which she liked to mix with satin, or silk chiffon. The skirts and arms were full, the waists cinched, the whole effect very pretty and soothing. She dabbled in gypsy skirts, fetching bolero jackets, camellias in the hair.

Meanwhile, Schiap, who'd struggled in the 1920s, made it into the big league with a single sweater. Her bow-knot sweater featured a black background with a fake white sailor's tie knit into the pattern, with matching knit white cuffs around the bottom of the sleeves. It was a cheeky takeoff at a time when clothes, especially haute couture, were serious business. *American Vogue*—Chanel's territory! —declared it to be an "artistic masterpiece."

Schiap started to design sportswear. She stuck zippers on the sleeves of ski jackets and created a bathing suit with a built-in bra. In 1934 she caused a sensation by designing a coat that fastened not with buttons but with a pair of small plastic hands. It seems the Muse had decided to pack her bags and move from Rue Cambon to the Place Vendôme, one street over, where Schiap opened a ninety-eight room atelier. The Ritz, where Chanel kept an apartment, opens out onto the Place; the back entrance near the Hemingway Bar is across the street from Chanel Modes. Schiap is said to have smirked, "Poor Chanel, she has to use the back door of the Ritz while I enter by the front!"

Schiap was a minx. She designed a collection of silk fabric whose pattern consisted of her press clippings. She foretold all the hoopla surrounding modern-day fashion week by giving her collections names. She launched a Zodiac collection, a Circus collection, and in 1939 she wowed 'em with a collection based on the Commedia dell'Arte that featured coats with harlequin patchwork and zippers with tiny bells. She loved classic cuts in wacky colors: purple, hot pink, and black. "Good design is always on a tightrope of bad taste," she said. Like Chanel, The Italian loved her maxims. She even floated her own Twelve Commandments for Women, and since this is a book with a quasi-religious title, I will include them here:

1. Since most women do not know themselves they should try to do so. (Duh.)

2. A woman who buys an expensive dress and changes it, often with disastrous result, is extravagant and foolish.

3. Most women (and men) are color-blind. They should ask for suggestions. (This coming from the woman who paired aqua and fire-engine red.)

4. Remember—20 percent of women have inferiority complexes. Seventy percent have illusions. (And 87.2 percent of statistics are made up on the spot.)

5. Ninety percent of women are afraid of being conspicuous, and of what people will say. So they buy a gray suit. They should dare to be different. (This

is a direct swipe at Chanel; Moses, the original commandment guy, would never have allowed himself to stoop to snark.)

6. Women should listen and ask for competent criticism and advice. (Had men also been advised to follow this commandment, the world would have been spared Dockers Relaxed Fit cuffed khakis with front pleats.)

7. They should choose their clothes alone or in the company of a man.

8. They should never shop with another woman, who sometimes consciously or unconsciously is apt to be jealous. (Stick with the kooky hats and leave the analysis to Freud.)

9. She should buy little and only of the best or cheapest. (Huh?)

10. Never fit a dress to the body, but train the body to fit the dress. (So SHE'S the one responsible for the practice of dieting to fit into the one size-too-small dress you bought for your high school reunion/best friend's wedding.)

11. A woman should buy mostly in one place where she's known and respected, and not rush around trying every new fad. (Excuse me? Shoe-hat anyone?)

12. And she should pay her bills. (Duh.)

It must have galled Chanel when a feature story in *Time* magazine, in the summer of 1934, stuck her house in the ranks of preeminent houses that were, nevertheless "not at present the most dominant influence in fashion," while Schiap was hailed as one of the "arbiters of the ultra-modern haute couture."

Perhaps worst of all, Schiap started dressing the most daring of the crème de la crème. Greta Garbo patronized Schiap, as did the Princess of Wales. Anita Loos, American author of *Gentleman Prefer Blonds,* was a Schiap fan, and so was celebrity clotheshorse and heir to the Singer sewing machine heiress Daisy Fellowes.

One could go on. And that's one of the chief problems with an archrival: One can go on. And on. And ON. AND ON. It can make you crazy as a sack of ferrets thinking about this person who's stealing your thunder, wandering around your old neighborhood talking trash about you, stealing your Little Darlings from under your nose. Remember Chanel's brilliant if slightly pretentious maxim about fashion being in the air, born upon the wind? Well the whispers that were born upon the winds of Paris were that women who were saucy, sassy, confident, playful, and individualistic were Schiaparelli women. Cautious little wrens who were afraid to make a fashion faux pas were Chanel women. One could go on.

Time passed. That's one thing you can count on, and one thing Chanel knew in her not-quite-Auvergnate bones. She was capable of lying in wait for many years. Schiap produced a military-themed collection in the spring of 1940, featuring camouflage-print taffetas. When the war intensified, Schiap fled to New York (Chanel was holed up in the German-occupied Ritz), then returned to Paris, then returned to New York, then back to Paris after the end of the war. By the early 1950s Schiap was unable to sell the world on her whimsy. I suppose two world wars in as many decades tend to make a confection like the Desk Jacket, yet another collaboration with Dali, featuring desk drawers instead of pockets, seem less than hilarious. She closed her house in 1954, the same year Chanel made her comeback.

Ha!

Did Chanel gloat like a maniac? She must have. But her public solution to coping with her first genuine competition was to act as if there was no competition, an attitude she'd honed during her *petite amie* days at Royallieu. Her refusal to lend Schiap a scrap of credence was absolute. Depending on how curled her lip was at the moment, Chanel referred to her as "that Italian artist who designs clothes" or simply "that Italian." When Chanel closed the House of Chanel in September 1939, the word on the street was that she could no longer stand playing second fiddle to Schiaparelli. Chanel claimed she was simply exhausted (she was), plus there was the tiny matter of another world war playing itself out on her doorstep.

All the best Chanel maxims are slightly opaque, koan-like. Perhaps her most famous one is "Elegance is refusal," which can mean any number of things, from refusing melted butter on your popcorn to refusing to pay too much attention—or any attention—to your rival.

8

ON MONEY

"Money is a good servant and a bad master."

Around about the time I realized that I was never going to buy a five thousand dollar Chanel jacket from the Spring '05 collection, or any other collection for that matter (which coincided nicely with the collapse of the stock market, and the realization that in all likelihood I would be trying to sell the few nice jackets I already owned at the consignment shop up the street), I landed a magazine assignment that put me six hours away from Paris by bullet train.

The sheer synchronicity of such an assignment—the e-mail from the magazine editor sailed into my inbox at the exact moment I was checking eBay to see if perhaps there was a nice mohair wool jacket circa 1964 on offer for forty-seven dollars that I'd overlooked—kept hope alive. Far from being over, my search for a Chanel jacket had just begun. Of course I would never find a magnificent piece of haute couture history on the Internet. What had I been thinking? Good for finding out-of-print books, boyfriends from middle school, and someone reliable to change your muffler (not to mention porn, which I won't, it being a different subject entirely), the Internet is a wasteland, and it's pure aesthetic folly to hunt for something as exquisite as a Chanel vintage jacket online. According to Coco, ". . . luxury lies not in richness and ornateness but in the absence of vulgarity. Vulgarity is the ugliest word in our language. I stay in the game to fight it."*

And yes, I too will stay in the game to fight it! And make no mistake, it is a fight . . . of sorts. Just walking the narrow streets of Paris, or trying to settle yourself gracefully onto the seat of one of the ubiquitous bentwood bistro chairs—squeeeeeeeek, please don't fail me now, aged wicker seat that has supported the weensy behinds of a million size 2 French mademoiselles since the reign of somebody or other—challenges my sense of self as a woman of normal, if not average, size for my height.**

In the smaller-than-a-phone booth water closets, with my enormous shoulders and shoes and my handbag that could hold multitudes, I can hardly turn around, much less sit, stand, and figure out the flushing device (the toilets of France have more methods of flushing than the nation does soft cheeses). I am Gulliver among the Lilliputians. I am a draft horse, plodding in nature, placid in temperament, with hooves the size of dinner plates, standing in the middle of a pasture full of fragile-ankled, tiny-nostriled, snorting, hot-blooded Parisian thoroughbreds.

I don't want to get all why French women don't get fat here. We know the drill: small portions, no snacking, smoke like a . . . French

---

One can only imagine what Chanel would make of the gaudy vulgarity of the Internet, with its flashing blinking ads, pop-ups, and spam.

**I am 5 feet, 9 inches; 143 pounds give or take; size 10, 36C, 9B; collar bones and cheek bones are in evidence, as are my hip bones when lying down on my back, provided I've not just eaten a bowl of popcorn, which tends to cause bloating.*

woman. My point is this: Take this *esprit de XXXL*, which the average American inevitably carries with her to Paris, and multiply it by, let's say, four (the size at which haute couture, like trees at the timberline, ceases to exist with the exception of a few straggling specimen around the edges), and you can get an idea of what it feels like going in search of Chanel in Paris.

Didier Ludot has two shops that sell vintage couture on the Galerie Montpensier inside the Palais-Royal, which hasn't been a real palace since Louis XIV spent his childhood there. It was turned over to a cousin of the Sun King in the mid-1800s, and he installed the shopping arcade. It was a hub of good-times, gambling, and general pre-Revolutionary debauchery. Then came the riots of the Revolution, then it was nearly burnt to the ground during the Commune of 1871, then it was further assaulted in 1986 when sculptor Daniel Buren was permitted to stick a field of black-and-white striped stone columns in the courtyard. During the reign of Chanel, Cocteau had an apartment here, and so did Colette.

Ludot keeps two addresses on the arcade. There is the open shop, and the shop that is open by appointment only. The open shop—presumably NOT the one where Reese Witherspoon purchased the vintage 1956 Dior that she wore to the Oscars—feels like a huge nest feathered with jackets, coats, day dresses, gowns, shoes, bags, and accessories that are vintage, but not vintage vintage. The appointment-only shop is where the treasures are: the half-century-old Dior, the Givenchy, the Jacques Fath, the Schiaparelli (her again!), and of course, the Chanel.

Just inside the unwashed masses shop, on the right, is a rack full of Chanel jackets and suits. Most hail from the pink and orange 1980s. They are Lagerfeld pieces. I scooted inside the door to have a look. The shop is no larger than an American elevator. (A French elevator holds one supermodel and her roller suitcase.)

I was nervous at the prospect of meeting Ludot—could anyone possibly be snootier than a Frenchman trafficking in vintage haute couture?—but when my friend and traveling companion Kathy and I entered his minuscule shop on the Palais-Royal, there was no Ludot, but rather a standard-issue French salesgirl standing in the middle of the store, i.e., three inches from my elbow. She wore red heels and a black dress of some space-age looking fabric cut to resemble a trench coat. Or perhaps it really was a trench coat. She had black hair and short crooked bangs and was neither pretty nor ugly but in the manner of all French women, uniquely *herself*.

The salesgirl inspected us, but otherwise said nothing. I wondered: Was she glad to be relieved from employing the high-end retail equivalent of the "Invasion of the Body Snatchers" warning bellow[*] popular in the luxury brand shops on the Avenue Montaigne?

Unsure what I mean by this abstruse pop-culture comparison? Stroll into, say, Fendi in your 501s and gas-station sunglasses and see what happens next. After passing the navy blue–suited security guard who nods as he opens the door for you, casting upon you a small

---

[*]*Every time one of the body-snatched sensed an unsnatched human in their midst, they'd point and emit a ghastly, and very loud, otherworldly howl.*

frown of pity, the salesgirls start cawing, "Bonjour Madame! Bonjour Madame!" It's not your imagination—they are sizing you up, and they don't like what they see (are those *cowboy boots* on your feet?). Their cries are shrill and urgent, notifying their confreres in the bowels of the boutique—past the sunglasses and handbags, the perfume and the lipstick (the stuff on which middle-class Americans routinely splurge in the hopes of feeling that they, too, are as chic as the sloe-eyed, long-limbed mistresses of Russian billionaire industrial magnates, or the Japanese), back in the land of the fifteen hundred dollar T-shirts and 10k frocks—that a large American wearing a Gap turtleneck and carrying a Fossil handbag, i.e., someone who literally has no business being there, is moving, moving, *moving* toward the . . . I daren't call it *clothing*, for that would fail to convey the degree to which I, a lowly wearer of J. Crew, am capable of contaminating the garments of pure fabulosity. . . . Bonjour Madame! Bonjour Madame! Now you are reaching toward a jacket. Bonjour Madame! You're actually . . . touching it! You're . . . taking the jacket off the hanger! Bonjour Madame! Bonjour Madame! Bonjour Madame! In the back, each fabulous piece has its own personal sales associate, who hovers, wringing her narrow hands, while you paw the merchandise with rough mitts that have not enjoyed the attention of a manicurist since the Bush administration.

But the salesgirl at Ludot's was spared all that. All she had to do was burn a hole in the back of my head with her stare. I asked her if she had any Chanel from the 1960s. "That is not here," she said.

"Awwww!" I said. "That's too bad, because you know, I'd really love to see some genuine Chanel. I'd love to own some, actually. One,

I mean, one jacket is what I'm after. I'd love a dress, but where would I ever wear a Chanel cocktail dress? I don't have that kind of life, not that I wouldn't want that kind of a life. I would. But really, I'm just interested in a jacket, or even just seeing a jacket. From the sixties. You know," I finished lamely.

"Not here," she said. The phone rang, and when she stepped behind the curtain at the back of the shop, I hauled Kathy out by the sleeve.

"We'll just call," she said. "We should have done that in the first place."

A French photographer friend told us we needed to make a proper appointment. The French have a high regard for writers (recall the jewel-encrusted sword you receive when you're inducted into the Académie Française) and Ludot would be more amenable to showing me the good stuff if Kathy rang him up, in her capacity as my fake assistant, and announced that I was an American journalist visiting from the United States, researching a book on Chanel, who would like to make an appointment to see some of his vintage pieces.

I'd complained to my French friend that this approach seemed so formal. Guess what? The French are formal. In our loud-mouthed, large-limbed, too-casual American way, Kathy and I had committed a faux pas by dropping in.

We regrouped and decided we would simply wait an hour, phone the shop using the special works-only-in-Europe cell phone I'd rented for the trip, and make a proper appointment. I assumed I was forgettable enough (not being French and therefore not being uniquely myself) so that when we showed up the next day, the salesgirl would never remember us, and Ludot, having never seen us, wouldn't know the difference.

We continued around the arcade, lingering in front of the window of Ludot's appointment-only shop (it was dark inside, all locked up) to see if we could guess who designed the red dress in the window. We moseyed up the other side. We stopped in front of one window and took some pictures of a row of mannequin hands, each one wearing an exquisite different-colored leather glove.

Twenty minutes later we came upon yet *another* Ludot shop, which sells nothing but little black dresses. I knew Monsieur Ludot had published a book about LBDs, as they're referred to in the business (making them sound related to WMD, which I suppose they are), but I was unaware of his matching shop, which sells a mix of vintage cocktail dresses and a line of his own dresses, inspired by the great designers of fifty years ago. Unlike his nestlike vintage shops, feathered with treasures, La Petite Robe Noire took the more predictably spare approach favored by your average luxury brand boutique.

We entered the shop and were stopped in our tracks by a weird sight: an adorable, ancient, walleyed, brindle-coated bulldog sitting in one corner, beneath a row of dresses.

At first we thought the dog was a statue, maybe a lawn ornament, stuck there beneath the skirts of two-thousand-dollar cocktail dresses as a hip visual joke. But when we bent over and peered beneath the skirts, we saw the dog was panting slightly. A gleaming string of drool dangled from the corner of his black lips.

He was real! We squealed, clucked, and cooed in the manner of dog enthusiasts the world over. His slobbery grin could have also been a grimace, and the walleye was also a little disconcerting, so we didn't stick our hands out for him to sniff, to see whether he might approve of a little chuck under the chin. But I did want a picture. I took the lens cap off my camera, then thought perhaps it would be polite to ask permission. I'd been so mesmerized by the dog, I hadn't noticed the salesgirl standing in the middle of the shop ... which was the same black trench coat-wearing, crooked-banged salesgirl from the *other* shop, the one who stood there and smirked while I gushed idiotically and supremely inelegantly about my love of Chanel. Was she an identical twin? A vampire? Wait was it her? Maybe it *wasn't* her. No, it was her.

"Si'l vous plait, je prend une photo le chien?" Oh wow, that was some crappy French there, but it is the only kind I know.

"Mais, non!" she exclaimed.

Then I did something that would ensure I would never have a meeting with Ludot, would never gaze upon his vintage Chanel-Chanels, would never even have the opportunity to contain my sticker shock when I saw that just like their baby Lagerfeld-Chanel sisters splayed open for all to see on eBay (the lapels, the tags, the careful quilting, the chain, the hem), Chanel-Chanels cost many thousands of Euros; I thanked her, then as I moved toward the door, I turned around, squatted down, and snapped a shot of the damn dog anyway—channeling my inner war correspondent.

"Madame!" she scolded, as we hurried out. She closed the door behind us.

Then she locked it.

In the same way it used to take fashion a few years to wend its way from Paris to Main Street America, it took the stock market crash of 1929 a few years to really work its way into Parisian society. By 1930 Chanel was the most expensive couturier in Paris, and also the wealthiest. Her empire consisted of about twenty-four hundred *premières* (the captains of Coco's army who translated her vision for everyone else, short for *premières mains*, or "first hands"); a cadre of seamstresses of different ranks and pay scales; dozens of *arpètes*, a beautiful word that basically translates as slave labor, the girls who under the guise of apprenticeship swept the floor, fetched coffee, and made sure the floor was free of needles; the stunning mannequins, who stood there for hours at a time while she fitted each garment upon their slender bods; the *vendeuses* and the *habilleuses* (the imperious saleswomen and their davening assistants). Chanel kept the lights on in twenty-six workrooms, most of which were devoted to reproducing various designs for Chanel clients, and a handful of "creating ateliers," where the new models for the new collections were painstakingly fashioned; she made a cool 120 million francs* a year.

Old francs. The new franc arrived on the scene in 1960. It was worth one hundred old francs. Now, of course, we have the Euro, which is worth . . . oh never mind, you get the point. It was a shitload of money.

Chanel's biannual showings were the hottest ticket in town. The food chain of those attending ran as follows:

1. Impossibly rich ladies—aristocrats, socialites, the occasional A-list actress or opera diva—who were the actual paying customers.

2. Fashion writers from *Vogue, Harper's Bazaar,* and the other glossies, in charge of spreading the word about what the impossibly rich ladies were eyeballing.

3. Buyers from the big department stores, Saks Fifth Avenue, Bonwit Teller, Macy's, and Altman's, who were watching what the fashion writers were noting, about which models the impossibly rich ladies were eyeballing.

4. Manufacturer's reps, there to purchase the most popular gowns, which they could then race back to the United States with and shamelessly copy and sell to the average woman.

Chanel was also the direct beneficiary of the insane trend for over-the-top masked balls that spread like chicken pox mid-decade. The Oriental Ball! The Grand Siècle Ball! The Masterpiece Ball! The Waltz Ball! Mademoiselle raked in the dough designing elaborate and ridiculously expensive costumes for the richest guests. For one masquerade hosted by Daisy Fellowes, in which everyone had to come dressed as someone they knew, Chanel made a small fortune creating gorgeous gowns for the lords, dukes, and earls who came dressed as the women in their lives (read: mistresses).

Not until relatively late in the economic day did Chanel begin to feel the pinch. In the early years of the decade she lost orders from American socialites, but she had more than one iron in the fire (Diversification! The sure key to financial success, according to all the money gurus) and still retained the patronage of the wealthy ladies of South America and India. It was rumored she took a hit in 1932 and was forced to cut her prices in half, but it didn't seem to take the bounce out of her step.

✵ ✵ ✵

Chanelore insists that because she was both a peasant and an orphan, Chanel didn't know anything about money.* This sounds like a rumor floated by Mademoiselle herself. Like world-class pool sharks and shrewd women who know the cloaking power of traditional femininity (see Chapter 9), it was to Chanel's best interest to be perceived as the provincial peasant she enjoyed believing she was, spending her days fretting over hem lengths and buttonholes. Janet Flanner, writing in the *New Yorker* said, "Though Chanel can make a fortune, she can't add

---

What does this mean, exactly? She didn't know how interest compounded daily worked? She was confused about how to carry a one?

straight; though she is brilliantly competent at the complexities of high finance, she can't do simple sums without an eraser."

But clearly she knew how to make money, how to spend money, and how to die having a lot of it. She also knew how to enjoy being a woman who'd made a fortune. At the height of her fame, her greatest delight was hiring the daughters of the aristocracy to work as underpaid salesgirls or mannequins. When she got wind of their dissatisfaction over the long hours and low pay, she'd tell them to do what any other gorgeous young thing would do—find a rich lover and use her charm to get him to pay the bills.

One of her attorneys, Robert Chaillet, once said Chanel possessed "the wily foxiness of a country horse trader." This makes it all sound so folksy, so easy. As if the ability to flatter the right people in the right way at the right time—a trait also attributed to silly females, let's not forget—is all it takes to amass and hang on to a vast fortune over the course of two world wars, a global depression, and in France, a workers' uprising.

Making and keeping a fortune requires (aside from luck) certain fiscal habits, practiced with monklike constancy over a lifetime. Not particularly sexy, but true.

Being and Staying Really Rich à la Chanel

Redefine the concept of money so that you can feel comfortable making it.

The extremely wealthy never want to be thought of as being in it for the dough. They consider themselves to be visionaries who revel in the freedom and opportunities their wealth affords them. They never want to be perceived as the king in his counting house, counting out his money. They're out climbing mountains, either real ones or metaphoric ones. In their heart of hearts they are not the greedy Bill Gates of Micro$oft, but the warm and fuzzy Bill Gates of the Bill and Melinda Gates Foundation, an "impatient optimist" who wants to stamp out polio and make sure every farmer in sub-Saharan Africa has his own dairy cow and working sprinkler system.

Chanel wasn't interested in what her money could do for others. True, she bankrolled Diaghilev's revival of *The Rite of Spring*, and occasionally bailed out the Ballet Russes over the years. She paid for Cocteau's rehab and also sent a monthly stipend to her mad poet, Pierre Reverdy. She never publicly acknowledged her brothers*— Lucien had become a shoe salesman; Alphonse sold newspaper subscriptions—but she did send them allowances until the day she closed the House of Chanel and perceived herself to be broke.

In this regard she was honest with herself about what her money meant to her. It was pretty much the Coco Show. But even *she* tried to pass off her love of money as being something nobler than it was. She said, "There are people who have money and people who are rich."

Presumably she was talking about herself as one of the rich ones

---

Julie and Antoinette died in 1912 and 1920, respectively. Not much is known about the events surrounding Julie's death; Antoinette had fallen in love with a young Argentinean who swept her away to Buenos Aires, where she died in a Spanish flu epidemic.

rather than one of the moneyed ones. But what made her feel so rich? Was it the lovers, who inevitably disappointed? Her one woman friend, Misia, who often drove her mad? Her Little Darlings, who rarely paid their bills on time and reconfirmed her low opinion of the highborn? Her racehorses? (Actually, you probably could make an argument for the horses; she felt they were nicer than people.)

Perhaps Chanel felt rich because her definition included knowing that on any given day she was winning the game, because the score was kept with francs. She allowed herself to like making money. She never felt that her own competence threatened her sense of herself as a woman. Money was more than her security blanket. It was her ongoing victory lap. It was the knowledge that she was dependent on no one, that she knew she could take care of herself. She reveled in it. She owned it. She flaunted it.

Those of us who aren't quite so clear on the role of money in our lives have generally been lucky enough to escape brutal childhoods, where by puberty we'd already been schooled in life's nastiest realities: People die; people leave; and the need for money rolls right on. We* tend to be like the woman interviewed in Liz Perle's *Money: A Memoir* who hates the thought of putting money in her savings account because it reminds her that no one is coming to save her.

But even if the prince is saddling up his white steed at this very moment, double-checking the stirrups and his investment portfolio, readying himself to gallop into our lives and fork over endless amounts

---

Are you fooled at all by this imperial "we" business? I'm talking about myself, of course, but maybe it applies at least a little bit to you, too.

of dough for our hair appointments, car insurance, and flatware, what if he's late? What if he gets here and changes his mind? What if we change *our* minds? That's the problem with waiting to be saved. You wind up with little choice in the matter. You get what you get. And if you have a temperament even remotely similar to that of Chanel's (exacting, luxury loving, and unwilling to settle), you're in a bind.

I could go on, but you should just read Perle's book and weep. Or you could adopt Chanel's somewhat disingenuous attitude toward money—it's fun to make, to have, and to spend—and forget the teeth gnashing altogether.

Desire little.

This heading is a little misleading. Chanel loved opulence and insisted on surrounding herself with beautiful things. After Chanel Modes began turning a profit, the first thing she did was get herself a Rolls Royce and a chauffeur (whom she insisted on calling her mechanic). Her place on Rue du Faubourg–Saint. Honoré, with its huge sylvan garden, was palatial. Her neighbors were the president of France and the British Embassy. The seventeenth-century Coromandel screens* for which she harbored a lifelong passion defined the rooms, all

---

Named for the Indian port near Madras from which they were shipped, these Chinese screens were created with methods dating back to the seventeenth century. Each wooden panel was coated first with clay before highly trained artisans inscribed complicated scenes of Chinese life, which usually included an egret. Often further decorated with jade, porcelain, and semiprecious stones, the screen was finished with forty layers of lacquer. Chanel's screens were legendary. Americans who do not traffic in high end Asian art know them as "room dividers" and can find cheesy ones at Pier 1.

furnished with Louis XIV antiques, crystal chandeliers, and heavy gilt mirrors. Her Simplicity Now! credo obviously didn't extend to her home decor.

But even though Chanel insisted on having the best of everything, she didn't insist on *having* everything. She could have easily floated a polo team, owned multiple cars, maintained a yacht and its crew. She could have invested in the paintings of Pablo Picasso and bought her own jewelry (instead she liked to take apart the precious gifts from ex-lovers and use the stones in her own designs). For that matter, she could have owned clothes. She wore nothing but that which came out of her workrooms, but there were periods in her life when she was so busy that she owned nothing presentable but two or three suits.

In fairness to all the profligate rich folk who manage to blow through their millions without breaking a sweat, there wasn't as much stuff out there to buy when Chanel was rocking Parisian society. I imagine she might have had a good time on a NetJet with Bill and Warren and their bowl of jelly beans, but such a thing hadn't been invented.

Chanel also said, "One must get as light as possible. Never let anybody else do anything for you that you can do for yourself." Forgive me, but I must call bullshit. This aphorism was a clear case of do what I say and not what I do. Since the moment Chanel arrived at Royallieu I'm sure not a day passed when a squad of servants wasn't on hand to do many things for her that she could technically do for herself. When she hit it big she had a butler, for crying out loud.

Aside from answering the door, what does a butler do, exactly, but boss around the rest of the help, which given Chanel's naturally despotic personality, should have given her immense pleasure?

Anyway, it's still a good point. Have a care about engaging a personal trainer, professional closet organizer, dog walker, color consultant, life coach, or, alas, the adorable shaggy-haired ne'er-do-well from down the block who offers to rake your yard. Gardening boasts all kinds of health benefits (which I can't recall at the moment).

Keep the villas to a minimum.

Given her income and her earning power, Chanel could have also owned a lot more real estate. This is where the well-to-do really prove to the world how many zeros they're talking about. Chanel could have easily sprung for multiple residences around Paris,* not to mention England, and St. Moritz where she liked to ski, and a sweet little pied-à-terre on the Upper East Side. But she had a horror of debt. "One should live within one's means," she said. "Otherwise there's always that extra thing bothering you. Never have a big house. Don't get caught that way."

At first she indulged herself, then lost interest in the large headache that accompanies the owning of property. The richer she got the more she downsized. The big house in Paris/chateau in Biarritz/ other random villas strewn about the French-countryside gave way

---

During the 2008 presidential election, it came to light that candidate John McCain owned at least seven properties, three of which were condos in Phoenix. Why even the richest person would require even one condo in Phoenix remains a mystery.

to La Pausa, her house in Roquebrune on the Côte d'Azur, and a suite of rooms at the Ritz, which slimmed down even further to a white, bare-walled chamber where she slept, and a few rooms above her showroom on the Rue Cambon where she entertained.

Just before the Germans marched into Paris in 1940, Chanel persuaded the Ritz management to build for her a tiny bedroom reachable from a small staircase off her sitting room; the room was as sparse as the one she had known at Aubazine, furnished with white bedding, a Russian icon given to her by Igor Stravinsky, and on her bedside table, the watch taken from Boy Capel's wrist on the day he died. It still kept good time.

Heed the wisdom of Jackie O.

Years ago I had the chance to meet Jackie Onassis at a literary event at the Kennedy Library in Boston. At the time Mrs. Onassis was a book editor at Doubleday. As a complete aside: The nibbles on hand were the standard Brie wheel, white wine, and mixed nuts. Nothing fancy. Then word came down from somewhere—in my memory I'm sure I saw one of the library guards talking into his wristwatch—and suddenly the crowd was abuzz. She's coming! She's coming! Away went the Brie wheel, away went the humble water crackers, away went the peanut-heavy mixed nuts, and out came the oysters, the skewered prawn, the beef tenderloin on rounds of rye with watercress. To this day I still wonder whether it was always like that at the Kennedy Library, with a fancy default buffet held in reserve in case one of the Kennedys showed up.

I was making small talk with one of the pages who had just gotten married, when Mrs. Onassis, who'd been standing in the clutch of people beside us, turned and, putting a hand on each of our shoulders, said,* "I like to share what I've learned with all young women I meet, because I wished I'd have known it at your age—never marry, never mix your money."

Chanel's desire never to weigh more heavily on a man than a bird echoes this advice. Because she made it her business to make her own money, she was able to have whatever sort of relationship she fancied with her lovers. She was never beholden, which always makes things so much easier. Everyone can relax. This also allowed her to remain friends with her lovers after the romances were over, because there was no accounting involved. Even after her affair with the Duke of Westminster ended she returned to him the blank checkbook he'd given her, having never written a single check on his account. Given that he was the richest man in Europe, this was sheer perversity on her part, but whatever.

Find a way to be generous.

"Tips are money invested for comfort," according to Chanel. I'm not talking 15 percent on that mushroom cheeseburger and Diet

---

*There must have been some polite chitchat prior to her simply barging in and holding forth, because just as everyone has always said, Mrs. O was the most gracious woman you've ever met.

Pepsi (20 percent if you've ever been a waitress).* Chanel routinely gave away free clothes to women who she thought would wear them well; and even though she was stingy with her own employees, she was famously generous with almost everyone else.

Once, when her mare won at the races, she made her jockey a present of a portable television. Then, remembering he'd just gotten married, she felt it was necessary to give his new wife something as well. So she rooted around in her jewelry box until she found an emerald, proclaimed it pretty, and sent it along with the TV. The emerald was easily worth several million francs.

Robert Streitz, the young American architect who designed her house in La Pausa, remembered showing up one day late for lunch. Mademoiselle would make the trip from Paris to the south of France once a month to check on the construction and in general order people around. She also enjoyed climbing the hundred-year-old olive trees she'd had transplanted from Antibes. Streitz's car had broken down on the way to Roquebrune, and he was forced to take the bus. He apologized profusely. Like a lot of people he was intimidated by Chanel's wit, her intelligence, and, yes, all that loot (she'd spent six million building the dream villa that Streitz designed, three times the amount the property cost); he imagined he'd get a good dressing down. Instead Chanel was sympathetic. She had the same kind of car sitting in her garage. When she asked

---

Chanel never carried any money with her aside from a roll of ten franc notes, believing that to tip any less was an insult.

her butler to retrieve the keys, Streitz thought he realized what she was about to offer and promised he'd get the car back to her within the week. But he'd misunderstood: Chanel was *giving* him the car. She never drove it anyway.

9

ON FEMININITY

"A woman who doesn't wear perfume has no future."

would never wade into this snarl of a topic, except Chanel had to go and say, "There is nothing masculine in me." (This from a woman who was competitive, aggressive, judgmental, fearless, confident, self-involved, and able to pretty much leap tall buildings in a single bound—all traits we associate with masculinity.) It presents several questions that give me the pinched-shoulder feeling I associate with existential questions that may be unanswerable. Such as: What *is* femininity anyway?

It's an odd time for the concept of femininity. Feminism is all over the place. Feminism you can have a discussion about. We live in a cultural moment where people are endlessly tussling about equality in the workplace, reproductive rights, and whether getting drunk on spring break and showing your boobs to the *Girls Gone Wild* film crew is empowering or not. Young feminists bitch out old feminists who sniff that if it hadn't been for the sacrifices of the bra-burning generation, feminism wouldn't even exist. Then there are the women who refuse to identity as feminists, while still claiming they believe in equality for women. (Who doesn't, aside from fundamentalist nut jobs?) The fires rage mostly on the Internet, but every season or so a book like Leslie Bennett's benign and sensible *The Feminine Mistake** appears and everyone gets all het up again.

But no one's really interested in *femininity,* per se. As a construct in need of some sprucing up, it's a nonstarter; we're perfectly fine writing it off as sugar, spice, and everything nice. This leaves us woefully short when it comes to a workable definition.

There appear to be two brands of femininity on display in the modern age. The first is the no-nonsense Focus on the Family version, which exhorts women to embrace their God-ordained femininity by being meek, gentle, submissive, pure, quiet, and sacrificial (even with divine help these traits are impossible to embody on a regular basis without the benefit of sedatives).

The second is the more mainstream, if equally difficult to achieve, *Sex and the City* model that suggests girly-girls are adorable, eternally horny shoe-fetishists whose primary passion in life is looking ready-for-their-close-up sexy while toasting each other with jewel-toned cocktails. Their careers exist only to explain how they can afford the clothes, shoes, jewelry, spa treatments, and twenty-dollar crantinis. There are men in their lives, but they discuss them as if they were orchid growers pondering the challenges of a particularly picky species that fails to thrive. These feministas

---

*The book induced hysteria by suggesting that women should have something to fall back on in the event their breadwinner hubbies lose their jobs (at, say, Lehman Brothers), leave them, or kick the bucket. Many women felt that Bennett was impugning their choice to stay at home with their children by mentioning that often life seriously sucks.

don't really love men—they love buying pretty things, and they love each other.

Surely this isn't how Chanel saw herself. This was the woman who said, "As soon as you set foot on a yacht you belong to some man, not to yourself, and you die of boredom."

Setting aside for a moment that Chanel was constitutionally unable to be meek, gentle, and—I'm sorry—*caring* in the way that femininity demands, she simply distrusted men. How could she trust them after her father dumped her at his mother's house, then disappeared? To even *think* of using femininity in the hopes of luring a man into taking care of her in exchange for her independence was impossible. She knew too well that it was folly to put her survival in the hands of anyone else. Her own mother took that route and where did it get her? Dead of a curable disease at thirty-two.

Chanel knew that the simple algebra of male-female relationships doesn't compute and never has. A+B does not equal B+A, which is what all the hubbub continues to be about. In traditional liaisons where She takes care of Him so that He can take care of making the money, if She is hit by a bus, He can still support himself and their children, albeit in a household of mismatched pairs of socks fished out of the dirty-clothes hamper and Dominoes on speed dial. But Denny's is open twenty-four hours a day, and no one ever lost a job because He failed to pick up the dry cleaning. Plus He can always get another She, and, if statistics are to be believed, more often than not He does.

If, on the other hand, He is hit by the bus, none of the things that She contributed to their partnership will put food on the table, which becomes apparent in about five hours, which is how long it takes the average human being to feel the stirrings of hunger. If this were as obvious as it seems, only women with trust funds would ever allow themselves to depend on someone else for their keep.

It's true that Chanel was not above coddling men in the time-honored feminine tradition. Until she was a very old woman, she dipped frequently into her toolkit of distaff wiles. But her beauty, charm, wit, and ability to pander were always used in the service of getting what she wanted, never because she imagined it was her feminine duty. She was the one (of the many, I'm sure) who said, "As long as you know men are like children, you know everything."

As for anything smacking of femininity expressed as a sisterhood of haute consumerism and endless gabfests, and running over to each other's apartments at two o'clock in the morning in the rain to comfort one another, I think I can safely say Chanel would have been horrified. While there is evidence she went antiquing with Colette, and she also allowed herself to be dragged along on Mediterranean cruises with Misia (although these don't technically qualify as girlfriend getaways, since Misia's husband, José Maria, was also part of the party), the idea that she would swing down the street arm in arm with her best girlfriends in a pair of towering strappy thousand-dollar sandals is laughable (not to mention against her philosophy of practicality and comfort).

Aside from Misia, Chanel didn't much like women—somewhat boggling since she devoted her life to dressing them and spent every working day among an immense sorority of female employees. Indeed,

Chanel's seamstresses were devoted to her, even though from all reports, working for her was like surviving the dressmaking equivalent of Outward Bound.

Not only was Chanel demanding, exacting, and stingy with the compliments, whenever someone dared ask for a raise, she was outraged and—here is actually a more typical feminine response— *hurt* that the worker in need would display anything but gratitude for being invited to work for the House of Chanel in the first place. Her attitude was this: I, alone, have created three thousand jobs for women who might otherwise be forced to take in piecework and live on the edge of poverty; how dare they ask for more (or, a vacation for that matter)?

All this changed in May 1936, when the Popular Front prevailed in France and the parliament was suddenly filled with Socialists and Communists who were inclined to think workers deserved more than the privilege of going blind hand quilting the stupendously beautiful suits designed by Mademoiselle. Throughout the spring and summer of that year, there was talk in the street about forty-hour workweeks, paid vacations, and the radical notion that people who worked for a living deserved a soupçon of respect, rather than scorn for having been born into a situation that required them to labor in the first place.

The workers of Paris went on strike. That summer many of them, on the trailing edge of middle age, saw the ocean for the first time. (The wealthy denizens of Deauville and the Côte d'Azur were appalled.) The women who worked for Chanel struck, too. Suddenly they had demands, like to be paid weekly rather than whenever Mademoiselle saw fit. They chained themselves to the front door and refused to allow Mademoiselle entry.

She was, predictably, furious. How dare they defy her? She fired three hundred of them on the spot. They couldn't have cared less. Eventually she was forced to give in. It was either that or skip next season's collection. She was livid. According to Chanelore, the reason she closed the House of Chanel three years later had nothing to do with the advent of World War II, it was simply to punish the employees who defied her. This move could be construed as an example of femininity, or simple childishness, which as we know is gender neutral.

I decided to consult an expert, Debra Ollivier, author of *What French Women Know About Love, Sex and Other Matters of Heart and Mind.*

FROM: Karen Karbo
TO: D. Ollivier
SUBJECT: Coco Loco?
Hey Debra:
I wanted to ask your opinion about something in the Chanel book that I'm having a hell of a time parsing. I'm writing a chapter on femininity, since Chanel actually once said, "There is nothing masculine in me." Like her buddy Colette, another self-made ball buster, she loved to talk about how womanly and feminine she was, all the while marching

through the world in a storm of competitiveness, bossiness, assertiveness, aggression, and outspokenness. Really, the only thing that seems quote unquote feminine about Chanel were her pearls and swooning adoration of cheesy romance novels. Otherwise, she was a five-star general in a little hat. She wasn't even particularly sexy in that smart-sexpot way that French men seem to appreciate. Then I got to thinking that maybe her brand of femininity WAS uniquely French and that I'm missing something. What do you think?

Cheers,

Karen

FROM: D. Ollivier

TO: Karen Karbo

SUBJECT: RE: Coco Loco?

My sense is that the qualities that contradict femininity for you or us American women—being competitive, bossy, assertive, aggressive, etc.—are less gender-specific in France. In fact as long as you're not "butch" or a man-hater, these qualities can actually be sexy in France. As long as men, flirtation, beauty, and seduction are part of your overall package, you can be bold/brash in France and still be perceived (or perceive of yourself) as feminine. Coco Chanel might not have been "ooh-la-la sexy"—she wasn't particularly sexy in that "sexpot way" nor was she a femme fatale in that mysterious/secretive way—but she had smarts and inner strength and never held back her desires. She might have been a "ball buster" but she also loved men and she loved their balls. She HAD balls, too, and she used them. That's sexy to French men. Smart is sexy. Inner strength is sexy. Asserting your desire is sexy. Being a seductress is sexy, even if you're a big, bold, in-your-face, unapologetic one.

So, for the French you can be that five-star general in a little hat, as you put it, and be simultaneously feminine. These contradictions can co-exist more easily in French culture than they can in our culture, where we tend to be more black-and-white about things. In France, being feminine suggests that you love men, that you're ready for men, and want them in the picture, even if you express attributes that we normally associate with men.

Amities,

Debra

Maurice Sachs, whom we will remember as the writer and bon vivant Chanel hired to outfit her library with first editions, once remarked that Chanel was "a feminine personage of a kind Paris had not known before." Which leads me to believe that not only was Chanel feminine in the traditional French way, she also put her own spin on it, which, as we know, was something of compulsion with her.

Femininity à la Chanel

Claim to be a lazy minx.

There is nothing more feminine than indolence. Étienne Balsan was amazed at the amount of time Chanel could spend in bed in the morning reading the newspaper. Chanel herself said, "I know how to be inert." After Chanel Modes opened and began printing money, the only evidence that she was ever inert was her suntan, which does require lying around in a meadow or on the beach between the hours of ten and two. Before Chanel, only peasants sported that healthy glow. (There is no evidence that Chanel invented the aluminum suntan visor for reflecting rays beneath the chin.)

Keep it to yourself.

Maintaining a sense of mystery is an outdated aspect of femininity, which can't be revived a moment too soon. However witty or charming you may be, no one wants to hear the details of your toxic-flushing diet, latest tooth bleaching, problems with vaginal dryness, or the energy-sucking he said/I said/he said/I said details of your last breakup. According to Chanel, "One shouldn't speak of oneself, or almost never. People should guess you." People can never guess you if you post the video of your gallbladder surgery on YouTube. TMI is never feminine.

Indulge your irrationality.

Because the hallmark of French femininity means an abiding desire to have "men in the picture," knowing how to interact with them in a low-maintenance way that requires neither endless midnight debriefings with loyal girlfriends nor a stack of self-help books cluttering the nightstand is key. Picasso said that Chanel had the most sense of any woman in Europe, and part of that good sense meant occasionally behaving as if she'd lost her mind, in the interest of reassuring the men in her life that she was irrational in a reliably feminine fashion.

In the interest of getting along, it makes it much easier on everyone when men behave as men are expected to behave, and women pretend to behave as women are expected to behave. Chanel learned this from training Balsan's yearlings, where success depended on reassuring the horse there will be no surprises. Squeezing him with your heels always means walk on. Sitting down and back in the saddle always means stop. In this way a horse comes to believe that even though he outweighs you by at least a thousand pounds, you are still the boss, and this comforts him. Horses, like men, are uncomfortable with unpredictability.

But unlike horses, men believe women are inherently unpredictable, which means—stay with me—that behaving unpredictably is predictable. Men know how to relate to you when you're irrational. Nothing pleases them more than a little unanticipated crockery hurling. When you're rational, they feel suspicious, then threatened. They start acting like a possum cornered in the back of garage, and soon the words *man hater* get bandied about and everyone is unhappy.

Most of the many lawsuits Chanel brought against Pierre Wertheimer (sexy überlord of Parfums Chanels) were filed not with the intention of settling any contractual matters, but to keep people talking about how she, the creator of No. 5—so slim and chic! so girlish!—was being swindled by a faceless corporation run by a ruthless titan of industry who took advantage of the fact she had no head for business (ha). In this way she made sure that the public loved her, and that Pierre had the satisfaction of complaining about her demands with the guys, while racing around calling special meetings of the board to placate her, and sending her flowers, and in all ways scurrying around trying to make her happy.

Worship at the altar of your own intuition.
Nowhere is Chanel's confidence in her own unerring intuition more on view than in her foray into jewelry. In the early 1920s she realized that feminizing menswear was about more than just making blazers, cardigans, riding breeches, and ski togs in smaller sizes. In culling all the available biographical material on Chanel, I haven't been able to find the exact Oprah Aha! Moment when she realized her plain sweaters and simple dresses were the perfect showcases for swags of costume jewelry, that instant it occurred to her that nothing said girly-girl like sticking a large sparkly brooch on the brim of your captain's hat.

Because Chanel was feminine in the French mode, she also needed to make a philosophical statement about why, during this time of roaring affluence, when even the least wealthy of her clients were Charlestoning beneath pounds of fine jewelry set with rubies, sapphires, emeralds, and all the rest, fake jewelry was more chic. According to Chanel, costume jewelry ". . . was devoid of arrogance in an era of overly easy luxury."

It will come as no surprise that Paul Poiret got into jewelry designing before Chanel. The poor man was Salieri to Chanel's Mozart, born to pave the way for her innovations. Of course Chanel put her own spin on it. Before Chanel, costume jewelry was mainly replicas of pieces of fine jewelry. She went one step farther and made sure there was no mistake about it: That enormous cross encrusted with knuckle-size "gems" swinging at the bottom of that heavy gold chain was as fake as it gets. The women who went gaga for her diamante flamingos and brooches set with brightly colored Venetian glass already *had* the real stuff.

Here I will stop and invite you to marvel at Chanel's influence during this decade. She decreed that timeless, beautiful—not to say one-of-a-kind and fantastically expensive—pieces were déclassé and vulgar and that instead women should adorn themselves with her jewelry, which was only timeless and beautiful because *she* created it. Of course it was also fantastically expensive. I'm reminded of the Woody Allen movie *Bananas,* where the first thing the rebel leader who becomes the dictator of the banana republic San Marcos does is order the citizenry to wear their underwear on the outside. Chanel had the same sort of influence.

Chanel had her own collection of dazzling fine jewelry, given to her by Boy Capel (his first lavish present was a diamond tiara; Chanelore says she was naïve enough to mistake it for a necklace), Grand Duke Dmitri, and, of course, Bendor, the Duke of Westminster. Dmitri introduced her to the long chains of gold interspersed with stones that became a hallmark of her look. Bendor would present her with an endless stream of priceless necklaces, brooches, and bracelets studded with Indian rubies, sapphires, and emeralds. While she always deferred to him in the presence of his posh friends, playing her spirited young Claudine card* and claiming to speak only French (while secretly taking English lessons, the better to know what everyone was saying about her), she then found it necessary, upon being presented with yet another breathtaking bijou, to take it apart before his very eyes, using the stones for something of her own creation, perhaps with poured glass. She loved nothing more than mixing fake stones and real ones just to, you know, keep everyone guessing.

Chanel hired aristocratic men who shared her taste for the "barbaric"** to manage her workshop and design for her. Étienne de Beaumont (who had snubbed her when she was still making hats) managed her workroom, and she hired a Sicilian nobleman, Fulco Santostefano della Cerda, to create the big, clunky bangles, jewel-encrusted cuffs, and ten-ton Maltese crosses that many of us mistakenly believed were popularized by Madonna.

Just when people were getting used to wearing those heavy arm-lengthening cuffs studded with knobs of poured glass, the Depression blew in and people started losing money and rich ladies felt lucky to have a collection of valuable, ostentatious jewelry to sell, Coco decided it was time to bring back diamonds (for example, the 7.5-carat oval brilliant-cut diamond that forms the centerpiece of the

---

*There is so much else we must give this woman credit for, must we also salute her for successfully passing herself off as gamine well into her forties?
**Defined here as ancient Greece, Byzantium, the early Renaissance, and anything that would have appealed to Dmitri, her favorite high-strung Slav.

18-carat white gold "Swing" necklace with 955 diamonds mounted on flexible gold threads).

Coco believed that "hard times arouse an instinctive desire for authenticity"—which admittedly doesn't sound like total bs—and that she was inspired by her new love for Paul Iribe, with whom she co-designed her Bijoux de Daimants collection.

Her more likely motivation was a recent commission from the International Diamond Guild. The masterpiece of Bijoux de Diamants was the Comète necklace that hugs the neck as if it were a wrist. The "comet" begins at the throat with a huge diamond-studded star; the tail is comprised of 649 diamonds that wrap around the nape, then continue over the shoulder where it ends just north of the cleavage. It's the most beautiful thing you've ever seen.

Pearls will set you free.

During World War II fake pearls were big business. Manufacturers took great pains to make them look as real as possible and devised a system whereby hollow beads of thin glass were filled with iridescent *essence d'Orient* (derived from the scales of a sardine-like fish called a bleak), after which the center was filled with wax and the glass mold carefully removed after the wax had cooled.

Perhaps you're a step ahead of me here; Chanel rolled her eyes, undoubtedly made some snarky comment that's been lost to time, and made sure her artificial pearls could be discerned as fake by a nearsighted octogenarian standing across the street. They were the pink-flocked Christmas trees of their days, phony and fun.

The truth about Chanel's bespoke femininity is that a woman can do or say whatever she wants as long as she's wearing pearls. Diamonds are a girl's good friend, but they are not her best friend. They associate too much with mobsters and oily Las Vegas entrepreneurs to be relied on to convey to the world that there is nothing masculine in you. And we won't even bother with their involvement in the so-called bling of stern, broad-shouldered hip-hop stars, who sport enormous million-dollar diamond stud earrings.

But if like Chanel you would ignore traditional feminine behavior while still enjoying the benefits of being considered feminine* (main benefit: escaping the label shrill and humorless, which was of enormous advantage to someone like Chanel, since at times she could be shrill and humorless), best to stick to pearls. Which is easier said than done. Consider: The chic and devastatingly feminine Jackie Kennedy was famous for her triple strand of pearls, but so was Barbara Bush. Pearls are tricky that way. The rule of thumb seems to be that the shorter the necklace, the greater the likelihood that you are going to look like a storybook grandma (even if you still have children in preschool). Which is not to say that a long rope of pearls is the obvious solution—too long and too swingy and you risk looking like you're on your way to a costume party dressed as a flapper.

---

*It seems any time I've sniffed around this issue I wind up reaching for Gloria Steinem's observation that all women are female impersonators; I'm doing it again here, but at least it's in a footnote, which I hope excuses me from plagiarizing myself.

The best way to wear them is to show your disrespect for their original form and purpose. Take a few long strands and sling them around your neck haphazardly. Wrap a necklace around your wrist. Chanel was known to wear half a dozen very long ropes and tuck them in her belt, which I can't in good conscience advise. After all, we are not Chanel.

Blame all your unhappiness on love.
See Chapter 4.

I don't know the percentage of women in Paris who get locked out of dress shops in the middle of the afternoon, but it can't be many. My giddiness at having knocked one out of the park on behalf of rebellious, ill-behaved Americans everywhere—I just wanted a picture of that adorable drooling old bulldog, is that such a crime?—subsided somewhat after Kathy and I tucked into the Starbucks* on the Avenue de l'Opera. To celebrate our disobedience Kathy bought us each a tall demi-écrémé latte. We drank it. We marveled at a man in a black turtleneck purchasing a small cup of black coffee and two

---

Yes, Starbucks, all right? Not a chic little art deco bistro known around the world for its croque-monsieur *and classic French whatnot, not a historic cafe that was a gathering place for revolutionaries, painters, existentialists, and their nutty women, but the Starbucks like the one on the corner by my house in Portland.*

small pancakes. Yes, FYI, they sell pancakes at the Starbucks on the Avenue de l'Opera.

It was clear that we would now never get past Didier Ludot's trench-coated gatekeeper and into the inner sanctum of the appointment-only haute couture shop. Kathy suggested that this being Paris, there were surely other places to find vintage Chanel, and as we wearily tried to figure out how to find a place that would welcome our shameless enthusiasm, it came to me: Chanel would have *never* jumped through these hoops.

She would have made her own.

And I was going to make my own.

I was, after all, the granddaughter of Luna of California, who forced me, at a young age, to learn how to sew. I hadn't made anything in years, but I was no stranger to the bias cut, setting a sleeve, or bagging a jacket. By sixth grade I already knew the secrets of copying a garment.

According to both my Paris guidebook and a Web site for textile aficionados, the best place for a good deal on fabric is at the foot of Montmartre, in the shadow of Sacre Coeur. Outside Métro stop Barbès-Rochechoart vendors sell barbecued corn on the cob from shopping carts, and it's a rough-and-tumble discount world. Shops spill out onto the streets with bins of T-shirts, plastic shoes, and household stuff. Most of the fabric shops snuggle in a pocket of streets clustered around the Rue d'Orsel. Their doors are flung open and bolts of fabric are displayed on the sidewalk, standing upright like umbrellas in their stands.

If there's one thing I learned from all that trawling on eBay it's that the Chanel jackets I liked best were those made in the loose nubby-or-not woven fabric called bouclé. We went from shop to shop asking whether they stocked this traditional Chanelian fabric. *Avez-vous le bouclé?*

No luck.

The only fabric for sale was for furniture and interiors—upholstery, brocade, chintz. We finally found some lonely pieces of bouclé in a shabbier-than-average shop, some black-and-white herringbone I could live with but didn't love.

On we went down the block. We found one street devoted solely to fabric for twirling and dancing, specifically belly dancing. Bolts of purple, turquoise, and pink sequined chiffon lined the walls. I despaired. How could it be that if you're a drum majorette with a sofa in need of covering there's a large selection of fabric for you in Paris but anyone else is out of luck?

Then we stumbled upon Les Coupons de St. Pierre, and just inside the door we found a table groaning beneath hundreds of folded three-meter squares of nothing but bouclé, and on a bottom shelf beneath the table was the perfect piece—deep mulberry blue woven with pink and a plummy brown, a browny plum, three meters for forty-five Euros, roughly sixty-eight dollars. We spread the fabric open like a blanket and inspected it for flaws.

At the cash register the small blond saleswoman patted the fabric and said, "Very nice . . . it's Chanel." I was over the moon. Yes, yes. Chanel! It is *just* like Chanel. That night back at the hotel, I noticed the name on the white plastic bag . . . Les Coupons de St. Pierre. What did *coupons* mean? Not *coupons* like grocery store *coupons*, obviously. Kathy dragged out her English-French dictionary. I'd assumed they just sold fabric in precut squares this way in France, but *coupons* means "remnants."

When the saleswoman said, "It's Chanel," she could have been speaking literally. My piece could actually have been left over from some House of Chanel collection from a few years ago. I thought I should go back and ask; I thought I should at least call to see where they obtained their remnants and whether or not it was really Chanel, or only Chanel-like. Then I thought, if this is being made in the spirit of Chanel, I'll just rearrange the truth, like she did. *She* would have gone ahead and claimed it was Chanel.

And so will I.

10

ON TIME

"There is time for work, and time for love.
That leaves no other time."

I f a genie popped out of a lamp and offered me one wish (down from three, times are tough all over), it would be to spend my days the way Chanel did. In my extensive research* there is no mention of her ever having shopped, cooked, cleaned, or argued with a laundress (she had someone else to argue with the laundress for her). Someone else wrote out the bills, had the Rolls serviced, and fed the dogs. There is no evidence that she did anything aside from boar hunting, fly-fishing, or yachting off the Côte d'Azur with her lovers, or working on her collections year in, year out, with the stamina of a cattle dog.

To work as Chanel worked required the schedule of a peasant not a socialite. She was never bowled over by the frivolities of society. In the evening she liked to stay in and get to bed early.**

Her solution to being seen around fashionable Paris was to

---

* *I manfully struggled through Paul Morand's* L'Allure de Chanel, *en français.*
***Translation: throwing huge fashionable dinner parties at home, from which she excused herself at two o'clock in the morning.*

befriend well-heeled beauties whom she would dress in her finest pieces and send out to the top restaurants and best parties. They were the unofficial emissaries of Chanel. She understood that sheer hucksterism was never the way to gain the attention of the ruling class. It was too tacky. Better to have someone else talking about you.

One of Chanel's favorite aphorisms was "Every day I simplify something because every day I learn something." The simplifying part is mathematically suspect—this would mean "simplifying" roughly twenty thousand things over the course of her career—and if there's one thing we know about Chanel, it's that she wasn't big on expanding her horizons once she'd formed an opinion. (The arrival of the miniskirt nearly gave her a stroke. "Fashion today is nothing but a question of skirt length. High fashion is doomed because it is in the hands of men who do not like women and wish to make fun of them," she squawked. And, "The mini skirt is dirty . . . one already collects too much dust and mud on one's legs in Paris, must one now have it on one's thighs?") Still, she did learn early on that time was the most valuable commodity and never went back on her belief that the only things worthy of consuming our time are work and love.

In one sophisticated swoop our problems are solved! Imagine: A devoted and harried PTA mom calls to ask whether you can help procure items for the annual school auction. You quickly measure the request against Chanelian standards of time allocation. Is it love or work?* Neither, so the answer is, "Megan, I would LOVE to help out but with all I've got going on at the moment, there is no time." Appreciate please that you are not saying "I don't have time"—after childbirth the most amazing thing women do is squeeze another hour or five out of every day—but stating the lack of time as an indisputable reality, like gravity.

Chanel may have loved the men in her life, but she was never as devoted to them as she was to the House of Chanel. Her workday didn't begin until noon, but then she was at it nonstop for a solid eight hours. On a rare day she nipped out for afternoon tea at Angélina on the Rue de Rivoli, but mostly she snacked standing up between fittings ("like a thoroughbred," she once described it).

In an average year during her heyday, Chanel made four hundred pieces for each of the two seasonal collections (shown in February and August). Every dress, every suit, every skirt, every coat, every evening gown, and every blouse was first constructed in toile, a muslin-like fabric in which she perfected each pattern. She famously had no use for preliminary sketches (handy, because she also had no drafting skills) and no urge to plot a paper pattern: "A sketch, a drawing—that's not the body. I don't sell bits of paper, and I don't charge for seats."

Chanel went straight to the part she liked best, and if I were pressed into choosing the best life lesson in this book, that would be it: Cut to the chase, don't waste time doing stuff that seems to be

Yes, I know it's work to get those bath shops and pizzerias to cough up gift certificates, but this offers an elegant way to get out of it.

essential to your life and business, just because other people do it. A smart friend once summed it up thus—why make nachos if what you really want to do is pick the browned shreds of baked cheddar off the cookie sheet? Just cook the cheese and be done with it.

Like everything else, of course, Chanel took this idea to impossible lengths and got away with it. She didn't even *pretend* to sew, as did her nonsewing competitors who felt their cred would suffer without maintaining the pretense that they occasionally ventured into their workrooms to run up a seam now and again. She designed her clothes directly on the types of bodies who would one day wear them.

Chanel relied exclusively on her *premières*—the saintly masochists who day in, day out listened patiently while she described her vision and issued her orders—without which her house would never have existed. But credit where credit is due: She had a knack for hiring talented people who could interpret her wishes and endure her personality. The *première* would hear Chanel out and then withdraw to the workroom, where she would oversee the creation of the first toile.

After the toile was cut and stitched by one of the legions of seamstresses, it was time for Chanel's League of Extraordinary Mannequins to get into the act. Here is where the real designing began, on the bodies of the girls who, according to my friend Alison's mom Ann, for a short time a member in good standing of the Extraordinary League, lived a sort of fireman's existence, lounging around the *cabine*, a mirror-lined back room, in their white silk kimonos, Merry Widows, garter belts, and silk stockings, playing endless games of Texas 'hold-em and taking turns cooking up vats of chili—ha ha.

They *did* however, spend their long days on call, sitting around, waiting to be summoned for a fitting or to show clothes to customers.

The mannequin was helped into the toile, and Chanel's work began. She wore a pair of silver-plated scissors on a white ribbon around her neck. Her assistants passed the pins. She thought nothing of taking a suit apart twenty-five times to get it right. Sleeves were her grand obsession; they could not fit close enough or high enough on the shoulder. Chanel could spend six hours on a single pair. The mannequin was forced to stand still while Chanel pinned, tugged, folded, patted, snipped, then ripped it out and did it all again. No one could rip a sleeve out like Chanel. She was without pity. She had no sympathy. A fidgeter would be told to get another job. As Claude Baillén writes in her memoir of knowing Chanel in her dotage, "Anyone who didn't see Chanel bent to her task like an insect seeking its pollen, searching, scrutinizing, fertilizing, has missed the essential part of her being."

Once the garment was perfected in toile, it was stitched up in jersey, tweed, crêpe de Chine, chiffon, satin, tulle, or stretch lace. Chanel chose every fabric herself. She was suspicious of any color that didn't occur in nature. She eyeballed buttons to make sure they didn't look like "poison chocolates." Then, the tugging, folding, patting, pinning, and snipping would begin again. She would perfect the piece until she hated the sight of it, then it was on to the next.

That's a bit of a downer, isn't it? The idea of working on something until you despise it? Chanel gets a pass because she is French and therefore expected to be pessimistic. Still, it completely flies in the face of the upbeat American advice, adapted from some ancient Chinese wisdom (which makes it seem timeless and therefore less ridiculous) that if you love what you do you'll never work a day in your life. It's such an inspiring sentiment I wish I didn't have to be the one to point out that as wishful thinking goes, it's right up there with the admonishment to make work play.

To excel at something the way Chanel excelled needs some kind of thorny and intractable psychological investment. To work ceaselessly at something, it really does need to hook into your psyche in some relentless way and offer a journey on the order of the *Lord of the Rings*, featuring seemingly insurmountable challenges, moments of wandering lost in the woods, the confrontation of enemies both internal and external, magic, luck, and a few hobbits to jolly things along. There are patches of work that feel like play—otherwise you'd give up—but it's not the most compelling part, the part that drags you forward and keeps you engaged. In any case, even people who literally play for a living, like those professional video gamers[*] who train ten hours a day and forgo any activity in which they might strain their thumbs, contend that "it's work, not fun."

But even Chanel needed a break from work and love once in awhile, and when Hollywood called, she answered. Making costumes for the movies was still work, but it wasn't the same as turning out her collections on the Rue Cambon. Either Queen Victoria or Mary Poppins said, "A change is as good as a rest," and I imagine that was

[*]*According to Lim, Yo-Hawn (aka BoxeR), the most successful professional computer-game player in history.*

what Chanel was thinking when she and Misia set sail for America in the spring of 1931.

There was something else. For years couturiers struggled with helpless outrage against the blatant theft of their designs. They formed a collective. They came up with a slogan, *Copier, C'est Voler* (loosely translated—copying is stealing). Paul Poiret in particular was enraged that his gowns were being whipped up by the dozens in cheap fabric in a factory somewhere and sold for ten dollars to the wives of petty bureaucrats. Chanel, alone among her brethren, not only didn't care, she encouraged copying. How else was she going to spread her style, and by extension, her philosophy? The rip-off artists provided free publicity, of which Chanel understood the importance long before anyone else.

The movies, with their global reach, were better than a thousand thieves. Especially in America, which from the beginning embraced the Chanel style with enthusiasm, any girl who could afford a quarter for a movie ticket would also be exposed to Chanel. Then she could trip out into the sunlight after the show, pop into her local clothing emporium, and buy a little jacket or skirt or even a satin gown (satin was the rage in the 1930s, and even Chanel succumbed) that looked like what she'd seen on the back of Greta Garbo, Joan Crawford, or Norma Shearer. Chanel was able to give her ideas away because the only place where they could still be executed with absolute perfection was in her atelier on the Rue Cambon, and the wealthiest women would always pay top dollar for that. And so they did, and so they do.

✳✳✳

To the degree that Chanel's childhood was textbook miserable, her adulthood was textbook charmed. Still, there were rough patches (lemons that she couldn't find a way to squeeze into lemonade, as she did World War I), and when Samuel Goldwyn invited her to California, she was going through one of them.*

It was finally over with Bendor, the Duke of Westminster. Like Boy Capel before him, without exactly breaking up with Chanel he'd managed to marry a lovely, well-titled nonentity who could give him both an heir and no backtalk. As much as Chanel's lovers loved her, showering her with jewelry and enjoying her spirit and individuality, it always came down to one thing: her refusal to give up the House of Chanel and their refusal to tolerate a wife who worked.

The idea that the woman who modernized feminine style and femininity itself would still be forced to choose between being a wife and being a career woman is quaint, retro, and—call me mad— enviable. Maybe it's my own exhaustion talking, but the cut-and-dried nature of it all is appealing.

Had Coco been born in, say, 1963 rather than 1883, she might have married a modern day Capel** and had three children—Nigel,

*It didn't hurt matters that he offered a million dollars to make the trip, about twelve million in today's dollars.
** I suppose she might have also married a modern-day Duke of Westminster who is still the richest man in England, but he's hardly the charmer Bendor was; recent pictures show him looking like a grown-up version of the portly Dudley Dursley, Harry Potter's muggle cousin.

Claire, and Elodie—who would be raised with the help of a string of unreliable nannies and/or babysitters, worrying every day whether she was spending too much time designing her collections and not enough time helping Nigel with his reading, or not enough time resetting those sleeves and too much time driving Elodie to gymnastics practice (surely Boy could drive her on the afternoons he golfed, couldn't he?), and, in the end, turning out nice, well-made frocks that were wonderful but not inspired (but they could have been!) while alternately overparenting and neglecting Nigel, Claire, and Elodie, who could not get enough of her divided attention when little, then would grow predictably into surly teens who despised her while begging her for an iPhone, whose problems could all be traced back to her failing to do something or other (she can't remember) and let's not forget, shall we, that Boy had expectations too, as does society, not to mention Chanel herself, that she would be not just thin, but also fit, not just fit, but celebrity fit, which involves triceps that can be confused with a steel girder, and abs off which you can bounce a quarter.

In short she would be, like the rest of us, obsessively involved in the exhausting, endless hour-by-hour recalibration of the work-family-life balance, running herself through what Slate.com writer Dahlia Lithwick calls the "sum-of-our-choices machine," which has the depressing effect of making us think that whatever it is we're currently doing, we should be doing something else.

But this is old news. We've been the bitches in the house for decades, angsty insomniacs who can never get it right (whatever "it" is). At any given moment it's obvious we've thrown ourselves under the bus of our self-generated complications. We suffer.

But as I write this, a really depressing trend is upon us. There's a new breed of hyperfertile, coolly confident, madly successful smokin' hot übermoms* who make the rest of us with one or two kids and a job look like kvetching multitasking lightweights. This woman is a chic, mad-cap, baby-making machine who's popped out enough children to man her own basketball team and has a sexy, good-humored husband and a messy, happy, chaotic home life tricked out with one or two nannies, a housekeeper, a kooky dog about whom a best-selling book can easily be penned in the wee hours of the night, between the third round of mind-blowing sex and five o'clock, when the baby wakes up. She always looks fabulous, if slightly disheveled, which only adds to her chic. The most irritating thing about her, which lurks in the subtext but which I will helpfully haul up into the text, is that she's a complete stranger to the sum-of-our-choices machine. She has no time for hour-by-hour recalibration; she can barely get the twins to practice—what sport do they play again?—on time!

Which is all a way of saying . . . what *was* I saying? . . . that in the same way I feel nostalgic for old-fashioned letter-writing and white popcorn (have you noticed you can only get yellow these days, and usually it's the microwave variety?), I miss the romantic notion that there are crossroads in life and one must make an irrevocable choice

---

Angelina Jolie, Sarah Palin, and Project Runway *finalist and blogger Laurie Bennett, please stand up.*

to go this way or that, then live with the choice without apology. Chanel chose to be Mademoiselle Chanel—rich, famous, absorbed in her work, admired, and sometimes quite lonely. Regrets? She had few (which, as she got older, she flung around in a manner that would have embarrassed her younger self, but never mind).

But back to the few years when Chanel went Hollywood. She was not a big traveler. She had La Pausa in Roquebrune, but mostly she preferred her own Paris neighborhood, even if it included a new, irritating neighbor, that Italian artist Elsa Schiaparelli, who was stealing both Chanel's press and her business.

She set sail for New York with Misia, who was recovering from having been thrown over by Sert for Roussy Mdivani, a leggy young Georgian "sculptress"* with whom Misia was also in love. For a time Sert and Misia shared Mdivani, who was a fetching and messed-up twenty-year-old gold digger. Then the triangle shifted about, and it was Misia and Mdivani who were sharing Sert. And finally, after Sert divorced Misia and married Mdivani, the geometry collapsed. As critic Clive James put it, "The triangle lasted for as long as Misia's pride allowed, plus a bit longer."

They traveled abroad the SS *Europe*. Chanel brought several pairs of her silver-plated scissors. In her luggage were six jersey suits and six evening gowns. Chanelore contends that after landing in

---

Roussy was one of the marrying Mdivanis, a tribe of ambitious siblings who fled Russia after the revolution to collectively marry, in no particular order, two heiresses, an Astor, the son of Arthur Conan Doyle, and silent-film star Pola Negri.

New York and spending a few days at the Hotel Pierre, they boarded a train headed nonstop for LA, stocked with champagne and caviar and painted entirely white.

Given the current reign of the celebrity stylist who gets paid stupid amounts of money to dress B-list starlets and sometimes fetch their daily Frappuccinos, Goldwyn's idea of dressing his biggest stars in the chicest clothes created by—as his head of publicity Howard Dietz introduced Chanel to the press—"the biggest fashion brain ever!" was ahead of its time. Still, the arrangement never quite took. "Talkies" had only recently caught on, and Chanel was never sufficiently starstruck to take a backseat to an actress. She found them to be nothing more than the puppets of the hammy producers, who reminded her of the market vendors of her youth.

In 1931 Chanel was assigned the task of costuming Gloria Swanson for her role as a frigid opera star in *Tonight or Never*. By now Chanel was back at world headquarters on the Rue Cambon. After having spent a few high-profile, publicity-jammed weeks in Southern California, neither Goldwyn nor Chanel saw any reason for her to hang around, and she was allowed to return to Paris. Swanson had been a huge star in the 1920s, but Chanel thought she was chubby. There was some diva-ing back and forth, and when it came out that Swanson was pregnant (in those days a career-ending scandal, not another opportunity to snag a magazine cover), Chanel ordered her top seamstresses to create a girdle-like garment made of elastic straps that would smoosh Swanson's belly flat. This went against Chanel's credo, of course, but she was determined that her gowns would look flawless. The movie, however, was a dud. Chanel's Hollywood days were numbered. Even though the Depression dragged on, and even though Coco Chanel and Samuel Goldwyn had no written contract, he never asked for his money back.

I am a veteran sewer of hideous jackets, created mostly in high school during long boring Augusts, between the day the new back-to-school issue of *Seventeen* appeared and the first day of school a month later. One piece stands in for the whole, painstakingly constructed yet ill-conceived lot of them—a rust, cream, and khaki–striped wool jacket with wide sleeves, raglan shoulders, and cork buttons. Forget, for a moment, that it made me look like the world's largest Incan woman. September is the hottest month in Southern California; indeed my friends and I routinely wore sundresses and huaraches until Thanksgiving. Which I always forgot when confronted with *Seventeen*'s gorgeous glossy pages of wool sweaters, kilts, kneesocks, and adorable knit caps.

Anyway, my point is this: When I launched into my DIY CIJ (Chanel-inspired jacket) project, I knew the accepted method for sewing a traditional jacket, but the Chanel jacket is no traditional jacket. A traditional jacket is essentially the meeting of two jackets, the inside lining (with the seams sewn on the outside) and the outside shell (with the fabric joined in the usual way). The jacket and the lining are stitched together with the right sides facing each other, then the lining is pulled through an opening in a side seam so that the wrong sides wind up facing in; with the addition of some pad-stitched hair canvas (to add shape to jacket fronts, collars, and lapels), interfacings and facings (which can be a bitch to wrestle properly into place) there you pretty much have it.

Until I tackled my CIJ, I took Chanel's mandate to simplify as a rule of style. Now I see that her philosophy of simplicity extended to her technique as well. Really, it's amazing that she was the first one to think of it.

The pieces of the jacket and the silk lining are cut out as one and machine quilted together in one-inch rows; the pieces are then joined by machine, and the lining hand stitched over the resulting seams. It's a method of assemblage a child with a gift for building things (my father, the son of Luna of California, who grew up to become an industrial designer,* always maintained that if you could design and sew a dress, you possessed the know-how to erect a skyscraper) might arrive at with no meddling help from adults.

Chanel famously did not excel at sewing and I wonder whether this is her doing, this unorthodox yet intuitive way of creating a jacket, or something her seamstresses arrived at. To wear it feels as if you're walking around in a luxurious personal quilt, with sleeves. Then, lest you forget you're not wearing the fleece in which you watch reruns of *CSI,* so comfortable are you, the hem chain gives the piece the heft it needs to hang straight and remind you you're clothed in a miraculous piece of haute couture.

He designed the hood ornament for the Lincoln Town Car and was on the design team that perfected the Frisbee.

It's nearly impossible in our age to consider the life lesson–worthiness of a subject without eventually turning a corner and running smack into Buddhism. Reimagining our quotidian tasks as a Zen exercise is pretty handy when you consider much of life consists of commuting to our cubicles where we perform jobs that are impossible to explain to anyone (even ourselves), then crawling back home to delete the spam in our inbox, scrub the grout in the bathroom, and, when Spring bursts forth, tug a weed or two. It really is comforting to imagine something elevated in all this monotony.

I was confident I could avoid Eastern wisdom altogether—the most mystical Chanel got was stamping gold buttons with her astrological sign—but then I made my CIJ and quickly discovered that aside from the machine-quilted lining, and the side and princess seams, every other part of it is hand sewn. The sleeves are hand stitched to the shoulders, as are the finished lining seams, as is the weight chain around the hem—all with an even, eyeball-straining fell stitch that joins the layers of fabric together in a manner that resembles a tiny, silken thread railroad track.

To imagine the seamstresses at the Rue Cambon patiently applying this expertise and love—for their work, for the design, for the piece, if not for the eventual owner—to every garment that passed through their hands* is mind-boggling. This is where the Buddhism

---

*By 1935 Chanel Modes had sold twenty-eight thousand pieces to women in Europe, Asia, South America, and the United States. If you feel compelled to do the fierce algebra, consider that she closed her house in 1939, reopened it in 1954, and died in 1971 while working on what would be her final collection.

comes in. I once read the explanation given by a monk about why every morning he and his brothers performed the same chores, sweeping and tidying rooms that were already spotless. Outsiders presumed that it was a way of practicing humility or a version of walking meditation or the adherence to some mystical ninja code of cleanliness. It was none of those things. Rather, the monk said, their humble rooms were made beautiful and hospitable because someone took the time to pay attention to them.

This was also the reasoning behind Chanel's hidden luxury, labor intensive beyond belief, and why she didn't care whether the world copied her designs. No one could duplicate the careful, perfect silken stitches that issued from her workrooms, the care and perfection that went into each and every lovely piece.

If you were to stumble upon a listing of my jacket on eBay, it might read:

One-of-a-kind Chanel-inspired jacket. Fabric is deep mulberry, plum, and rose bouclé remnant from last year's Chanel collection, or maybe not, depending on whether or not creator misinterpreted saleswoman at lovely Montmartre fabric shop. Single breasted. Fully lined with blue-gray silk lining purchased from a very nice shop in Portland, Oregon. Four pockets in front. All with functioning buttons—or will have functioning buttons. Owner currently torn between purchasing some genuine Chanel buttons with interlock-

ing Cs that don't really match the rest of the jacket, and also seem a little over-the-top, given that this is a Chanel-inspired jacket and not the actual item. Fringe edges throughout. Signature chain on the bottom inside. Brand-new.

11

ON LIVING LIFE ON YOUR OWN TERMS

"The answer isn't to climb down but to rise higher."

There are pictures of Coco Chanel made by Horst, Christian Bérard, and Cecil Beaton taken several years before she closed her house, during the height of her rivalry with Elsa Schiaparelli. She is fifty-two or fifty-three, wearing black or beige, her flat chest festooned with swags of pearls. I'm thrilled to report that she was never more beautiful; and it's not just me. Writing in her lavish *Chanel and Her World: Friends, Fashion and Fame,** Edmonde Charles-Roux says, "At age fifty-five, Gabrielle Chanel was in the prime of her beauty. Her features, like her figure, had reached their ultimate refinement. And never had she dressed with more invention or greater perfection." Only a French person could say this without feeling compelled to say that she also looked phenomenally young, which she did not, given all that smoking and sunbathing (decades before SPF No. 5).

*Published in 2005 in the United States by the Vendome Press, the paper stock is so heavy and satiny, you want to find a way to frame it, wear it, or perhaps frost a cake with it.

Exhaustion never looked so good. Despite Chanel's always astonishing amounts of energy, the workers' strikes of 1936 and her ongoing feud with Schiap and her purple parachute dresses were beginning to take their toll. Clients who experimented with a little Schiap hat or sweater were treated as persona non grata and never forgiven.

Chanel's growing exasperation with her aging clientele could be heard in her remarks, given in an interview with *Vogue* in 1938, which strayed from her normally pithy aphorisms: "At forty women used to exchange youth for elegance, poise, and mysterious allure, an evolution that left them undamaged. Now they measure themselves against the very young with defenses that can only be described as ridiculous."

Chanel was middle-aged, and because we live in less genteel times, I'm just going to turn all the cards over—menopausal. No one even knew about hormones until 1905, and thirty years later the dots still hadn't been quite connected. Estrogen and progesterone weren't discovered until the late 1920s, and their role in contributing to the mood swings, crankiness, irritability, snappishness, and unchecked hostility in middle-life* women was unknown. Although scientists, particularly the Dutch, were feverishly at work trying to make sense of these odd chemicals the body produced whose sole purpose appeared to be to effect change in another, far-flung part of the body, people basically still held the opinion left over from Victorian times

---

A term coined by baby boomers that sounds less depressing than "middle-aged."

that there were three stages of a woman's life—childhood, breast-feeding, and death—and if you weren't dead by the time the breast-feeding ended, your "monthlies" eventually stopped and you went insane. In any case, no one would have ever known whether Chanel was struggling with menopause, because she was pretty much always irritable, snappish, etc.

Was this then also a factor in Chanel's throwing up her hands and closing the House of Chanel in the fall of 1939, three weeks after France, in response to Hitler's invasion of Poland, declared war on Germany? Somewhere a doctoral student in women's studies has the answer, but according to Chanelore it was her belief that another war would spell the end of fashion. She was wrong.

One day she was open, and the next day she let her entire staff go and closed and locked the doors. The closure took Paris completely by surprise, especially because the war—at least as far as Paris was concerned—didn't begin in earnest for nine more months. The *drôle de guerre* or "phony war" commenced—sure there was bad stuff going on in Danzig, but what did it have to do with the average Frenchman?—and after the initial shock of being at war yet again with Germany wore off, it was Parisian business as usual. Blackout curtains reappeared on the windows, but Maxim's was still crowded with the fashionable set, there to enjoy its famous mussel soup. The only thing different at the Ritz was the lack of extra pillows; they'd been quietly removed from the guest rooms and sent to military hospitals in anticipation of the arrival of the soon to be wounded.

The fashion houses that had initially followed Chanel's lead cautiously reopened their doors. Eventually Madeleine Vionnet would close her house, and Schiaparelli and Mainbocher would flee to America, but Cristóbal Balenciaga, Jean Patou, Edward Molyneux, Nina Ricci, and others soldiered on, producing smaller collections that were no less amusing for their size.

Blue was big that season; leather was already being rationed, so coats were shown with extra-big pockets in which women could carry things they normally tucked in their handbags. Some designs meant to help the war effort sounded as if they were created especially to be satirized. From a press release of the period: "A few models in the new collection deserve special mention '. . . . *Offensive* brings together a printed silk blouse and a fairly long skirt made in a woolen fabric in the same tone, a short jacket with printed silk lapels, and a small bag of the same material for the gas mask.'"

Still, the windows on the workrooms on the Rue Cambon remained shuttered. The boutique stayed opened, but after the current stock sold out, the only thing for sale was No. 5, which sold like hotcakes until the liberation and beyond. Chanel simply refused to play.

On June 14, the day German forces took Paris and declared it an open city, Chanel fled with everyone else, having paid her bill at the Ritz through the end of summer. She wound up in Pau, in the south, the place where she and Boy Capel had fallen in love. There she ran into Étienne Balsan, now an old married man who still loved horses more than anything else. After all this time they were still friends; years before he'd used his influence to help

Chanel buy a piece of property for her nephew André Palasse. But no sooner did she arrive than on June 22 the French asked for an armistice with Germany. Paris would be occupied, but Chanel was able to return home to the Ritz, which she did without a moment's hesitation.

When we think of what it means to live life on our own terms, it's generally in regard to our personal dealings. It translates into not taking crap from anyone and is embodied in the cares we lose when we decide not to be something but to be someone. It all sounds good—heroic, defiant, self-actualizing. There is nothing we admire more than a rule breaker, except when the rules we break are the ones of basic human decency. If part of the terms we live by involves refusing to acknowledge an atrocious world war being waged, if not on our doorsteps, at least in our neighborhoods, a war that will affect everyone we know, and leave no one unchanged, we risk turning from a rebel into an unbearable solipsist. Chanel found World War II to be uninteresting, vulgar, and inconvenient, and so she turned her back on her city, her community, and her industry. The walls are very thick at the Hotel Ritz, and behind them she sat. It's hard to tell how she felt about her own behavior during the occupation of Paris, but the world was less enamored of her, and rightly so.

There was much to admire about Chanel's character, and I hope that, like the market hawkers from whom she descended, I've done a good job laying out my evidence in an entertaining and pleasing manner and sold you on the more difficult parts of her personality. When it comes to her behavior during World War II, however, the best I can offer in her defense is that few of us have ever been in her position, so who are we to judge?

The lessons to be learned from Chanel's choices fall into the category of cautionary tales. There's no escaping a few home truths, a species of reality check I've always wondered about. Is a home truth a basic truth about ourselves? Or is it a truth only someone at home (i.e., our mother) dares to tell us? The definition I like most is "a key or basic truth, especially one that is discomforting to acknowledge." I like it because it doesn't say who is most discomforted, the teller or the recipient.

Home Truth No. 1: There is a price to be paid for maintaining the sliver of ice in your heart.*

Chanel fell in love with a Nazi. Hans Gunther "Spatz" von Dincklage's mother was English, he never wore a uniform, and his business was mostly PR—trying to convince the French that the Germans weren't psychopathic warmongers, but regular guys who appreciated France and French culture so much they wanted it for their own—but nevertheless.

Graham Greene once said that the heart of every artist comes equipped with this.

The falling-in-love part is forgivable. Spatz was handsome, charming, erudite, *younger*. The human heart is the most wayward beast that roams the known world. That, and at the war's outset no one was handing out copies of *The Rise and Fall of the Third Reich.** First there was the phony war, when nothing much happened, then the Germans marched into Paris, Hitler sped in for a quick spin around his conquest, then France signed the Armistice. It was war business as usual. Everyone who didn't flee prepared themselves to hunker down and wait it out.

Jewish persecution began a mere two days after the occupation in the form of required registration with the police, but it wasn't until a full year later that Parisian Jews began being deported. The information age was a long way off. There was neither Huffington Post nor Drudge Report to refresh obsessively every fifteen minutes. There was no television. Radio was embraced, but it could also easily be ignored. If you so desired, you could shut your door to the world, and that's what Chanel did.

Early on the Germans decided to treat Paris as Epcot, a cultural theme park for the officers and higher-ups. Jean Cocteau was named director of the national theater, and Chanel's old pal Serge Lifar, the one-time principal dancer of the Ballet Russes, became director of the Paris Opera Ballet. The racetracks reopened, and German officers were admitted for free. Occasionally Chanel

---

*A huge (twelve hundred-sixty-four pages) and hugely important history of the Nazi party by William Shirer that is stomach turning in its portrayal of Hitler's monstrosities.

showed up at the ballet to see Lifar, but mostly she stayed home. She started taking singing lessons, and she and Spatz threw small dinner parties at her apartment at the Ritz. More people than you might imagine didn't see anything wrong with Chanel's choice of lovers.

I wonder what this boneheaded refusal to acknowledge her role as a Parisian, a French woman, a citizen of the world cost her, if only in emotional terms. Consider: The armistice had been signed in the Compiègne forest on the exact spot the Germans had surrendered in humiliation to France in 1918, a stone's throw from Royallieu, the scene of her young adulthood, where she'd lived with her first lover, developed her taste in reaction to the overdressed lollipops around her, conceived the idea of a career in couture, and learned to ride and love horses. The Germans had occupied Royallieu during the First World War, and after the Battle of the Marne it was converted into a hospital. During this new war it would be converted into an internment camp for resistance fighters and, eventually, a transit camp for Jews. Colette's husband, Maurice Goudeket, would be interned there. And yet, there's no evidence that she who was so famously passionate and feminine was saddened or appalled or even filled with the cheapest sense of nostalgia.

Chanel famously refused to live in the past, or admit it even existed. Even when it came to her dresses (as she referred to everything she designed whether or not it was actually a dress), once she had created it, she forgot about it. Once it was perfected and out the door, she never sought it out, never sought out the woman who purchased it, never gave it another thought.

The problem with this, of course, is that as you get older the past starts piling up like dirty laundry in a fraternity house. The future shrinks, the past grows, and to refuse to develop a relationship with it is to cut off increasingly larger chunks of who we were and what our life has meant.

Home Truth No. 2: There is a price to be paid for willful ignorance.

As the war ground on, sides needed to be taken. Even though Paris still went about its business as a cultural playground, no one could ignore the implications of the German defeat at Stalingrad.* All the nonsense about "Franco-German intellectual exchange" petered out as one by one the salonnières, the fashionable women who hosted arty gatherings that often included charming German officers, closed their doors. It turned out that the resistance movement was more than an idle rumor.

Although Chanel still would not return to her atelier, other designers kept producing new work. Chanel had been uncharacteristically wrong—fashion rolled right on. But the customers had changed. Most French society ladies had been impoverished by the occupation; the new customers were black marketeers (the so-called butter-egg-and-cheese people, because they'd finagled ways to avoid the rationing) and the wives of high-ranking German

---

Still cited as the worst battle in human history, with a death toll of 1.5 million.

officers.* They bought new frocks by the armful and created a market for high-end ready-to-wear. New boutiques popped up to fulfill their nouveau shop-til-you-drop appetites.

Chanel refused to discuss the war. She insisted it was not worth her attention. She and Spatz even spoke English to each other (apparently the secret lessons she took while dating Bendor were a success). Her wardrobe diminished to two suits and three blouses, or perhaps it was three suits and two blouses. Anyway, she was no longer the chicest woman in Paris.

For a time in 1942 she lived with Spatz at La Pausa. I was going to discuss how she interceded on behalf of a Russian scientist friend of her architect, Robert Streitz (to whom she gave her car all those years ago), who'd been snatched by Gestapo, in an attempt to illustrate that she wasn't utterly deaf to the atrocities of the time, but I simply can't bring myself to do it.

Really, I want to shake her and ask, "Coco, what the *hell*?"

Did it never occur to her that if respected scientists were being arrested willy-nilly by her lover's boss, that just maybe it was time to admit that she'd been thoroughly slimed and get rid of him? Was being with a *Nazi* really better than being alone? She, who so famously (and hypocritically) said, "I've always had the courage to go away . . . a woman hasn't all that many ways of defending herself. She has to go."

So why didn't she? Because she was a selfish git.

---

*The argument could be made on Mademoiselle's behalf that her stubborn refusal to reopen her doors was evidence of her own style of patriotism—if she couldn't continue to sell her creations to French society, she certainly was not about to do business with German women or French collaborators.

Home Truth No. 3: Once it's clear you've messed up, don't make it worse for yourself by making up lame excuses.

France was liberated in the summer of 1944, and within days of General de Gaulle's triumphant reentry into Paris, everyone who'd rubbed shoulders with the heinous occupying Germans had some 'splaining to do.

"You are permitted in time of great danger to walk with the devil until you have crossed the bridge,"* according to the old Bulgarian proverb, meaning that during times of war people need to be forgiven some of their indiscretions, poor judgment, and bad behavior. Of course, the liberating army is never quite so philosophical, and the members of the Free French were no exception. Unless you were a card-carrying resistance fighter and had the passwords and decoder ring to prove it, chances are you were guilty of some form of collaboration, however minor.

Lifar was hauled in immediately, accused of entertaining Hitler and his troops in his capacity as director of the Paris Opera Ballet. He claimed he was only doing his patriotic duty by keeping French ballet alive. They released him, and he hid for three weeks in Chanel's closet at the Ritz.**

Cocteau managed to escape without arrest, then felt so guilty he developed a chronic skin rash that made him look like a chicken in full molt.

---

*I'm not sure what bridge they mean, but you get the point.
**He eventually surrendered; his punishment was a year's forced retirement.

The designers who'd kept their houses open, faithfully turning out collections that featured showy full skirts, strangely gathered bodices—making the resultant shelf-bosom look like a bolster pillow—and fur coats, hatched excuses more creative than those of a clever sixth grader caught with his hand in his mother's purse. Some said they created these peacockish fashions simply to defy German restrictions and regulations (nonsensical, since the only people who were able to afford couture were the Germans and their cronies). Some said they were intentionally creating over-the-top costumes to make the collaborators who purchased them look foolish (that really showed them).

Chanel made no profit off the war, nor did she flee to the safer shores of America. Still, her sin was impossible to overlook. The French may be famously blasé in the face of the sexual indiscretions of their politicians, but they took a dim view of women sleeping with the enemy. Indeed whenever I'm tempted to romanticize the French Resistance, I remember the glee with which they ferreted out women who'd succumbed, shaved their heads, painted swastikas on their foreheads, and paraded them naked through the streets.

Chanel was arrested in September and presented to the Committee of Public Morals. Lifar was there the day the two gentlemen came to take her away, and he remembered that she left with her head held high, silent and imperious. She was furious and frightened, but she wasn't about to make a fool of herself. Nor did she make up any stupid excuses for what she'd done.

She was held for several hours and then released. To ensure she wouldn't be rearrested, in a signature move that was more classically Chanel than any rope of pearls or quilted bag ever would be, the first thing she did upon her return to her shop was to place a sign in the window announcing that in celebration of the Allied victory she was giving away bottles of No. 5 to every American GI who walked through the door. Giddy soldiers lined up around the block, guaranteeing that if the police came for her again they'd have to get past her own personal army.

In the end Mademoiselle escaped punishment. According to Chanelore her old friend Winston Churchill, whom she used to allow to beat her at cards at La Pausa, interceded on her behalf. She departed for Switzerland without another word.

Do Not Hurry, Do Not Rest
—GOETHE

What did Coco Chanel do all those years in Switzerland? This has always confounded me. The woman was a workaholic. She loathed Sundays because her workers had the day off. And yet she spent eight years in exile. Accounts exist that have her reading novels and fashion magazines in her room in the morning, making and keeping appointments with her doctors in the afternoon, then shopping and going out dancing with friends. Where, I ask you, does a gang of ladies in their sixties go dancing in Lausanne? I try not to imagine a down-on-its-luck dance hall where Chanel and her old Swiss cronies shuffle around in the smoky gloom to the strains of a scratchy Piaf record, after they've had a ball snatching up cheap handbags (yes, you read that correctly) at Bazar Vaudois. Really, it's just too depressing.

Throughout Chanel's life the lone family tie she'd consistently maintained was with her nephew André, to whom she showed her affection by purchasing real estate. In Switzerland she bought him a house and vineyard, an apartment, and a villa in the forest. Sometimes she visited him, but she preferred to keep to her old lady habits.

And what about Spatz? What was he doing while she was out on the town?* He'd scurried out of Paris with the retreating German army and then showed up again in Switzerland, where he and Chanel resumed their mystifying relationship. It lasted a few more years, then suddenly he was gone, finally "retiring" (like living off Chanel in her Swiss abode wasn't retiring enough?) to an isolated Mediterranean island where he devoted himself in his declining years to the occult and, um, erotic sculpture.

I want to imagine that the moment Chanel set up housekeeping in the quiet land of excellent chocolate, cuckoo clocks, and secret bank accounts, she was already plotting her return. She was always a genius at gauging the prevailing cultural winds, at watching and waiting until the time was right, and that's what she did. Or, perhaps

Oh, who cares.

part of the secret deal Churchill brokered on her behalf was that she would stay away for as long as it took for the dust to settle.

It took awhile. Three years after the war ended, in 1948, during a visit to Paris she was approached by a young photographer for *Harper's Bazaar,* Richard Avedon. He wanted to do her portrait. Not many people did. Really, no one wanted anything to do with her. This was no glamour shot; he posed her outside, against a wall, looking beautiful and slightly ruined in a black dress with a white collar, three long ropes of pearls tucked into her narrow black belt, beneath an old poster that said *Pourquoi* Hitler? Clearly she had no idea where Avedon, in his brilliant heartlessness, had posed her.*

Paris was different. Society had lost its sheen. The link between the artistic and the affluent that had been forged during Misia Sert's reign was permanently broken. Marcel Proust and his deep attraction to fancy costume balls and being petted by society ladies he would then lampoon in his novel were long gone. Instead the darkly handsome and brooding Albert Camus penned his brilliant and depressing novels, and cafe society was colonized by dour existentialists (yes, Jean-Paul Sartre, I'm talking to you) who hogged all the good tables at La Flore.

Chanel was a relic, an old woman whose name was kept alive by a perfume in a simple bottle.

Time passed. She read her fashion magazines. Timing was everything.

Avedon spared Chanel the humiliation and didn't publish the photo until after her death.

Enter Christian Dior. The line that roused Chanel from her Swiss idyll was originally called Corolle (translated roughly as "petal" in French and reflecting Dior's belief that he was creating a silhouette that made women look like flowers), but Carmel Snow, the Anna Wintour-like commandant of *Harper's Bazaar*, dubbed it the "New Look." Indeed, indeed. The skirts were long and voluminous and demanded in some cases an astounding sixteen yards of fabric, the waists were pinched, the bodices boned, the hats reminiscent of the pastry platters Chanel had worked to overthrow so long ago.

It was a gorgeous, voluptuous, and completely impractical look. But the world had just survived a war, and the first thing that happens after the ration books are tossed in the trash and the men return home is that women's fashions get silly. I'd love to know if this is true in other cultures—that in years of peace women are drawn like zombies to fussy, impractical clothes in which they can barely move.

Chanel couldn't believe it. Hadn't she already fought and won this battle? Yet here we were again! In bustiers! In dresses that required hip padding and petticoats! In long-line corset-bra combos that crushed the ribs and pressed the breasts into a torpedo-like shape only a weapons manufacturer could love! She simply couldn't bear it.

Rumors swirled that Chanel was going to attempt a comeback. Aside from launching a new round of lawsuits against the Wertheimers over the perfumes (by now it had become her hobby and her sport), she did nothing. The decade turned, and she received word that Misia had died in Paris. She boarded the next plane and when she arrived, she shooed everyone from Misia's room. She ordered a bowl of ice cubes, which she used to smooth her friend's wrinkles. (How did she know to do this?) She made up her face, dressed her in white, and slipped her best jewels onto her wrists and hands. When the mourners were resummoned, they saw the redoubtable Misia as they remembered her, elegant to the end.

The lessons of a comeback, especially one launched at seventy, could constitute a book all their own. It's one thing to strike out as a young woman, beautiful and full of energy and lacking the wisdom to know better, but imagine Chanel—old, disgraced, all too aware of the cruel vicissitudes of the fashion world, and utterly alone. On the upside, by the time you're seventy you've been through it all and the biggest thing you have to lose is your pride (no small thing if you are Chanel). Your complete lack of a long-term investment in the future imbues you with to-hell-with-it courage you might not otherwise possess. It's why people over a certain age are always saying if you have your health you have everything: To launch something this ludicrous you need the stamina. By then Chanel was living exclusively on the profits of No. 5,* but she didn't have the capital to relaunch herself. The only person she knew with pockets deep enough to support such a venture was "the gentleman from Neuilly" as she referred to Pierre

---

*A full account of the complicated legal wranglings that resulted in this arrangement can be found in Axel Madsen's Chanel: A Woman of Her Own. It's both a juicy and nourishing read—like a good steak—and all Chanel lovers should read it anyway.

Wertheimer, her true husband. In order to get his attention, she let it leak that she'd cabled *Harper's Bazaar* editor Carmel Snow about the possibility of having any new models she created mass-produced by a New York manufacturer.

The eternally debonair Pierre was a distinguished gentleman only five years younger than Chanel. Still, she could jerk his chain as if he were a sixteen-year-old boy hoping to get laid. Mass-produce new Chanel designs in New York? *Mon dieu!* Chanel was Paris. Chanel was chic. How the haute reputation of No. 5 would suffer if she was perceived as being anything else.

Pierre and Chanel had been more than friends and more than enemies for decades. He felt happy to be leveraged yet again, and, given the length of their relationship, would have taken offense had she done it any other way. He funded half of her comeback collection, writing it off as publicity expenses for the perfumes. (*Lesson:* **If you're lucky, you get old enough so that your enemies become your friends, if only because you are a repository of their history and vice versa. Appreciate it. And if you're crafty like Chanel, use it.**)

She reopened 31, Rue Cambon, had the tarnished mirrors redone and dusted off the gilt chairs. She hired two forewomen, a fitter, and one mannequin, a beautiful debutante named Marie-Hélène Arnaud.

The newspapers indulged in breathless speculation. Fashion writers started spinning some Chanelore, saying she was coming back in order to pump up flagging sales of No. 5. They didn't know (yet) that the New Look had driven her mad, or that this sort of huge risk, similar in scope to the one she took before the First World War when she insisted on moving beyond her hat shop and making her simple suits up in lowly jersey, kept her blood moving, kept her alive. As old as she was, there was still a girl inside who loved to gallop through the forest on a two-year-old stallion. (*Lesson:* **No matter how old you are, that girl is always in there.**)

She told reporters she was returning because she was bored, because she was only happy when she was working, because "I prefer disaster to nothingness." All the beautiful black-and-white photos of Chanel made by Beaton and Bérard during her reign between the wars were unearthed and splashed about, fueling a trend for stories that glamorized the days before the Second World War. She trusted none of it. (*Lesson:* **Never believe your press.**)

Balenciaga, upon learning of Chanel's plans to present a collection in February 1953, sent her flowers in the shape of a heart and quipped to the press, "Chanel is a bomb. Nothing can defuse her." No matter, Chanel was back in fighting form, calling the flowers suitable only for a coffin and quipping "Don't be so quick to bury me." (*Lesson:* **The older you get, the sassier you can be; somehow a bitchy middle-aged woman is bitter and pathetic. Then, you get old and suddenly you're appreciated for your verve.**)

February 5, 1954—the showing at the House of Chanel was the hottest ticket in town. The place was packed with anyone who was anyone; editors from the French, English, and American editions of *Vogue* and *Harper's Bazaar*, rich society ladies from Chanel's past, young fashion journalists who sprawled on the bottom steps of the hallowed staircase, never guessing they would be made to pay for their bad manners.

The audience was silent as the first mannequin paraded past in a black, collarless suit, followed by a heavy navy blue jersey suit with two patch pockets, worn with a sailor hat. Where was Chanel the rebel, the iconoclast, the woman who was going to single handedly overhaul fashion?

It was a disaster.

The French press was sneering and merciless. They said she was tragic. They said she was stuck in some interminable year in the 1930s. They called her old and out of it. She was devastated, but undeterred. She had faith in what she knew to be true.

I'd wager that the debacle of her first show only fueled her determination. She crowed that they were trying to kill her off, which is preferable to being treated as if you were already embalmed. She wasn't treated with the reverence and respect you'd accord someone who was once beloved but no longer mattered. She was still in the game, and she knew it. She went back to work even though few orders came in. She viewed it this way: No orders means no distractions; we can make an even better collection for next time. Indeed she pretended to be delighted. And maybe part of her was. She always liked a fight. (*Lesson:* **Fuck 'em.**)

Chanel estimated the creation of her February collection would cost fifteen million francs; it wound up costing thirty-five million. She'd burned through Pierre's investment and was flat broke. One day he came to visit her at her atelier, presumably to offer his condolences and assess the damage. She was working and made him wait. Didn't the old coot see that she could not possibly be interrupted?

It was not a good day for Chanel. Even though she was, as usual, immaculately turned out in a sand-colored suit, pumps, and the hat she wore to hide the spots where she was going bald, her arthritis was giving her fits. Still, she sat, she stood, she knelt, she crawled around on all fours. Hour upon hour, while Pierre sat and watched, she tried to force her fingers to press, tuck, fold, and gather the fabric. It was torture.

When night fell, he walked her back to the Ritz. She began to complain to him about her hands, her fatigue, then stopped in the middle of the narrow street, halfway between the front door of 31 and the back entrance of the Ritz, shook her head and said, "Of course, we will continue."

Pierre, moved by who knows what—her courage, maybe, her stubbornness, or that fact that he, too, was getting older—said, "Of course we will."

And then, according to Chanelore—although I'm willing to rewrite history and say it was true—she did the most amazing thing. Coco Chanel put her hand on his arm and said, "Thank you."

Pierre Wertheimer called his partners and told them to give her as much money as she needed.

Chanel designed another collection, then another one. She didn't jettison what she knew to be true just because people didn't understand her (yet again!). She knew that women still had to get dressed. They still had to sit down, slide into cars, and raise their arms. After the war, women had been sick of scrimping; they enjoyed the sheer lavishness of the New Look, the revived fuss made over dressing. But at the end of the day, it was still a nuisance, and Chanel knew it. They would get sick of being constricted, and they would come back to her. It took some time. The French, in the usual forest-for-the-trees scenario, were too enamored of the few thousand women who still indulged in haute couture, too respectful of their own snooty traditions, and too wigged-out over the possibility that New York, and not Paris, might now be the fashion capital of the world. American women, who were always sympathetic to the modern, the unfettered, and the sensible, brought her back.

By the time Chanel had launched her comeback, every design house needed to be able to sell their patterns to the mass manufacturers of Seventh Avenue, or eventually close their doors. Chanel had known this as early as 1931, when she was returning from Hollywood and stopped in New York to see what the garment district was all about. During a quick visit to Klein's department store, she saw she was being mercilessly ripped off and understood immediately that this was the price of having your style embraced not just by the wealthy, but by the world.

She'd always contended that style was merely fashion until it reached the street, but she'd honed her own understanding of this.

It appeared there were several "streets"—an average street in a middle-size city down which a secretary might walk in her $20 Chanel-like straight skirt and easy-fitting jacket; the high street, where the wives of professional men lunched and shopped in their

$150 copies purchased at Bonwit Teller; and the fanciest streets of all, Madison Avenue or Wilshire Boulevard, where women with trust funds, married to captains of industry, strolled in their $500 ensembles made by their own dressmakers.

By 1955 the New Look was getting old, and by 1957 it was over, even before poor Dior himself died unexpectedly in October at the age of fifty-two.* Chanel was back, dressing new socialites and the New World celebrities, movie stars. Grace Kelly, Elizabeth Taylor, and Rita Hayworth all wore Chanel.

She had lived long enough now to suppose she'd enjoyed many last laughs; one of them was her new stable of mannequins. Aside from a few commoners, and a sassy Texan named Suzy Parker, they were all daughters of the French upper class, the granddaughters of the women who had snubbed her all those years ago. Claude de Leusse, Jacqueline de Merindol, Mimi d'Arcangues, Odile de Croy— thoroughbreds all. Like an old tycoon who marries and remarries a series of trophy wives for the youth and vigor they confer upon him, Chanel loved the company of her mannequins. They made her feel so young. When she heard the rumor that people thought she was gay, she laughed with delight. "At my age?"

Marlene Dietrich, her old customer, looked her up when she was in Paris. Dietrich, now in her fifties, was being paid a fortune to phone in a cabaret act at the Sahara in Las Vegas.

"Why have you begun again?" asked Dietrich.

---

*According to Diorlore he either died of a heart attack, while choking on a fish bone, or else after some particularly energetic sex.

"Because I was dying of boredom," said Chanel.

"You too?" said Dietrich.

※※※

By 1960 Chanel was back on her throne, where she would miraculously reign for another eleven years. It was all Chanel, all the time. American women routinely stood in line to purchase copies of Chanel suits. In 1964, Orbach's sold two hundred in a single afternoon. Like tiny dogs and British queens, Chanel looked poised to live forever. She'd outlived most of her friends and old loves, most of whom were younger than she.

Grand Duke Dmitri died of tuberculosis in 1941. Like Boy Capel before him, Étienne Balsan was killed in a car wreck in 1953, the same year Bendor died of heart failure. Her beloved poet Pierre Reverdy died of natural causes in 1960 at the Benedictine Abbey of Solesme, where he'd lived as a lay monk since 1930, and Cocteau joined the heavenly choir in 1963, having just learned of the death, also of heart failure, of his old friend Edith Piaf. Igor Stravinsky outlived Chanel by three months. Serge Lifar survived her as well, but he was young enough to be her son.

The depressing thing about writing about someone's life is that at the end you're left with the nearly impossible task of making their decline and eventual death seem uplifting rather than the full-throttle downer it always is. Dorothy Parker said, "There are no happy endings," and this is what she meant.

In her final years Chanel lived to work and complain. In 1969 she passed up the chance to see Katharine Hepburn play her in the all-singing, all-dancing Broadway musical, *Coco*. She begged off, citing her health, but she was terrified of seeing her life splayed out that way and perhaps afraid, too, that she would be feted and celebrated and applauded by the audience, and the cast and crew, which would force her to soften her views, a certain danger since it was her roiling bad mood that kept her going.

She was snarkier than ever. She disparaged everyone. Of one designer she said his brocade dresses made women look like armchairs from the front and old Spaniards from the back. She said the industry was being killed by pretension. She called her fellow designers pederasts and women haters. She said the student protesters of 1968 should be arrested and put to work building roads. She said Brigitte Bardot was beyond help, fashionwise, because she was a slob. She railed against America as a country of cheap goods, a place where the citizenry was "dying of comfort." She said all of her old friends were witless and diabolical and merely out to use her.

She was lonely.

And the obvious lesson here is straight from Ralph Waldo Emerson: "The only way to have a friend is to be one." And, I might add, try to be less insufferable.

Chanel presented what was to be her last collection in August 1970. She was eighty-seven. The miniskirt had had its run—as she predicted, no woman could stride through the world baring twelve inches of thigh for long. She showed a version of what she always showed: the perfectly proportioned knee-length suits with well-tailored jackets, both short and long, and a matching silk blouse and an embroidered black evening dress with a lovely neckline and ropes and ropes of pearls.

On Christmas Eve, several weeks before her death, Chanel No. 19 was released. After all these years Chanel was sick of smelling like everyone else (i.e., like Chanel No. 5), and she worked for a year with Bourjois perfumer Henri Robert to create something brand-new. Once a week he would present himself at the Rue Cambon with samples, and once a week he would be turned away.

Named for the August day nearly ninety years earlier when Chanel was born in the poorhouse in Saumur, No. 19 is described alternately as strange, sublime, elegant, and confident. It's considered "difficult" by perfume standards, the balsamic green galbanum* in near conflict with the duskiness of the iris. No. 19 is both green and powdery, with top notes of lemon and the galbanum; rose de Mai, jasmine, and ylang-ylang at its heart, an almost masculine mix of vetiver, sandalwood, and oak moss at its base.

Chanelore tells us that around the time of No. 19's release, it may have been that Christmas Eve, Chanel was either dining at the Ritz, and strangers stopped by her table to ask the name of her haunting, beautiful scent, or else she was in the street, at the end of the day,

---

*An aromatic gum resin that grows in the mountains of Northern Iran, galbanum is an ancient ingredient. In Old Testament times it was used in incense to represent the willful, disobedient sinner. First-century naturalist Pliny the Elder claimed a drop of it could kill a serpent.

and she was crossing from the Rue Cambon to the Ritz, and a man reached out and put his hand on her arm, and as she whirled around, determined to give him a piece of her mind, he smiled and asked, what is that astonishing fragrance you're wearing, mademoiselle?

12

ON ELEGANCE

The Gospel According to Coco Chanel

1.

I n the beginning was Coco, and Coco was fashion, and Coco said to the multitude, fashion is not something that exists in dresses only. Fashion is in the sky, in the street; fashion has to do with ideas, the way we live, what is happening.

And the clothes that were elegant were the garments made by Coco, who is Chanel. The cardigans, belted and unbelted, the cardigan coat and day dress, the day dress in beige jersey, the black jersey two-piece evening dress, the evening dresses in white silk net and black Chantilly lace, and in red silk also, to be worn with shoes of red silk and gold piping.

And the suit of tweed, herringbone, or bouclé, with edgings of contrasting jersey or braid, and the quilted lining of silk, and the blouse of silk that matches the lining, and the skirt that is neither long nor short, but perfect in the eyes of the stylish.

And inside the garments made by Coco, who is Chanel, all is beautiful, a sight to behold, because elegance means a thing's as beautiful on the wrong side as on the right, and luxurious is a garment that is pretty whether it is buttoned or unbuttoned.

And then Coco, who is Chanel, said art is imperfection, disorder is the symbol of luxury. But the garments that issued from the palace at Cambon were perfect in the eyes of all who had eyes to see them, and the multitude declared Coco a great artist, and she said, you do not understand, I am a dressmaker.

2.

And the rich women of the city that is Paris, some of whom were married to philistines, some of whom were the whores of the mighty, some of whom were the daughters of men of industry, thinking they understood, desired to be dressed by Coco, and they came in haste to the palace at Cambon, and she would not see them, and they did not understand, although they purchased her garments until there were no more. And they declared themselves to be fashionable.

But Coco said fashion fades, only style remains, and I am style.

She said, style is elegance, and elegance does not consist in putting on a new dress. An elegant woman should be able to do her marketing without making housewives laugh, for those who laugh are always right. And still the rich women did not understand, which did not prevent them from buying her cuff bracelets.

And Coco said that elegance is refusal, and the rich women not just of the city that is Paris, but of all the cities of the world both far and wide, understood this to mean rising from the table without partaking of sweets, and refusing all foods between meals, so that their bellies might remain flat.

And Coco said that it was good, but that was still not what she meant.

3.

Coco said, when I speak of elegance I am speaking of luxury. Luxury must remain invisible, but it must be felt. Luxury is simple; it is the opposite of complication.

Luxury is a necessity that begins where necessity ends.

Some people think luxury is the opposite of poverty. It is not. It is the opposite of vulgarity. Luxury is the opposite of status. It is the ability to make a living by being oneself. It is the freedom to refuse to live by habit. Luxury is liberty. Luxury is elegance.

4.

And then the modern times were upon us, and luxury was no more, according to Coco, who is Chanel. Women went to dinner in dirty pants and a man's shirt. Luxury was replaced by squalor. And Coco said fashion is always a reflection of its own time, but we forget this when it is stupid.

But comfort has its forms. A skirt is made for crossing the legs and an armhole is made for crossing the arms, therefore tear from your body any garment that does not allow you to walk, to run, to lift your arms, for it is inelegant.

And if a dress is shaped like a bubble, a barrel, or any other form that does not conform to your body, you must tear it from your body.

And if the dress is well formed but also brings to mind a bed-sheet, a linen napkin, or a tarp, which may also be used to cover the vessel parked in your driveway, you must tear it from your body.

And if you were to wear pants that rest so low upon the hips that that which is called a muffin top is created, you must tear it from your body, and if you wear pants that rest so low upon the hips that upon sitting the cheeks of your buttocks are revealed, you must tear it from your body, for it has offended me, also the multitude who pass behind you.

And if, upon opening the door of the small room that is your closet, you find that your garments have become tired before your eyes, and there is no goodness in them, remember that this is neither the time nor the place nor the hour to allow yourself to be filled with the spirit of creativity, nor fall into temptation.

For remember, a bandana is not a top, a long shirt is not a dress, a short dress is not a shirt, and shorts worn over tights are reason to banish you from the kingdom of style forever.

For the truth of Coco, who is Chanel, is true now, and in the world to come, that it is better to possess a few elegant pieces in which one always feels at ease, than anything that resembles the garments of the former Spice Girl who is Victoria.

5.

And Coco, who is Chanel, lived until she was nearly the age of Abraham. But before that Sunday in the first month, that is January, she ascended into her small room, which was in the hotel that was the Ritz, a small room not unlike the room she knew as a child in the orphanage that was Aubazine, and she laid down upon the bed in her suit, in her blouse and pearls, and removed her two-tone pumps, and placed them beside her bed, and then understanding that her hour had come, called out and said, "This is what it is like to die," thereby dying as elegantly as she had lived. Before that time she gave an interview to the magazine that was called the *New Yorker* in times of yore, and is still called the *New Yorker* in these times, and she said:

> *I must tell you something of significance. Fashion is always of the time in which you live. It is not something standing alone. But the grand problem, the most important problem, is to rejuvenate women. To make women look young. Then their outlook on life changes. They feel more joyous.*
>
> *Women have always been the strong ones of the world. The men are always seeking from women a little pillow to put their heads down on. They are always longing for the mother who held them as infants. Women must tell men always that they are the strong ones. They are the big, the strong, the wonderful. In truth, women are the strong ones. It is just my opinion. I am not a professor. I speak my opinions gently. It is the truth for me. I am not young, but I feel young. The day I feel old, I will go to bed and stay there. J'aime la vie! I feel that to live is a wonderful thing.*

ACKNOWLEDGMENTS

Although most writers feel as if they're alone in pushing their rock uphill, it takes a village to write a book and always has. My deepest gratitude goes to the stylish, savvy, and endlessly patient Hilary Black, who was there at the beginning. Eileen Cope at Trident Media Group is a literary agent par excellence, whose unswerving faith in me and my work means more to me than she'll ever know. For their hard work, excellent taste, and good humor, I owe a debt of thanks to Lara Asher, Jennifer Taber, Katie Sharp, Sheryl Kober, Bob Sembiante, and Gary Krebs.

An extra special thanks goes to the incomparable Chesley McLaren, a gifted fashion designer in her own right, whose cheeky, elegant illustrations captured the Chanel esprit.

I would also like to extend my gratitude to Chelsea Cain, who demonstrated it's not only possible, but desirable, to wear Chanel with the proper pair of torn jeans; to Alison Brower who introduced me to her mother, Ann Brower, one of the members of the League of Extraordinary Mannequins during Chanel's comeback years; to Carol Ferris, for looking into Chanel's stars and reaffirming what we all knew about this fierce Leo; to Kathy Budas, partner in crime and traveling companion extraordinaire; to Marcelline Dormont, who knows where all the good things are in Paris; to Liz Ozaist, who graciously allowed me to shoehorn in some Chanel research while on assignment for her in France; to Debra Ollivier, for her wisdom regarding all things French; to Kim Dower, an old and dear friend who knew me when and offers sound advice now; and also to Kim Witherspoon and David Forrer at Inkwell Management, for their gracious support over the years.

※※※

I am also indebted to the many authors who carefully and with extraordinary skill parsed the life and work of Coco Chanel. My most well-thumbed titles include: *Chanel Solitaire,* by Claude Baillen; *Chanel: Collections and Creations,* by Daniele Bott; *Chanel and Her World,* by Edmonde Charles-Roux; *Mademoiselle Chanel,* by Pierre Galante; *Coco Chanel: Her Life, Her Secrets,* by Marcel Haedrich; *Chanel: A Woman of Her Own,* by Axel Madsen; *L'Allure de Chanel,* by Paul Morand; *Chanel: Couturiere at Work,* by Claudia Schnurmann and Shelley Tobin; and *Chanel: Her Style and Life,* by Janet Wallach.

Other books that helped me understand the times in which Chanel lived, loved, and worked include *Bendor: The Golden Duke of Westminster,* by Leslie Field; *Misia: The Life of Misia Sert,* by Arthur Gold and Robert Fizdale; *Them: A Memoir of Parents,* by Francine du Plessix Gray; *The Forgotten Generation: French Women Writers of the Inter-War Period,* by Jennifer E. Milligan; *A Life of Picasso: The Triumphant Years, 1917–1932,* by John Richardson; *Grande Horizontales: The Lives and Legends of Four Nineteenth-Century Courtesans,* by Virginia Rounding; *A Dash of Daring: Carmel Snow and Her Life in Fashion, Art and Letters*, by Penelope Rowlands; *Cocteau: A Biography*, by Frances Steegmuller; and *Paris Fashion: A Cultural History*, by Valerie Steele.

Many thanks go out to the helpful and generous folks who schooled me in Chanel couture, especially those at Les Arts Dècoratifs and the Musée de la Mode et du Textile, the Metropolitan Museum of Art, the Philadelphia Museum of Art, the Academy of Motion Picture Arts and Sciences, madisonavenuecouture.com, and *Threads* magazine. Judith Head of Josephine's Dry Goods and Marla Kazell, dressmaker extraordinaire, deserve a round of applause for their guidance and good taste.

A big, heartfelt American *merci beaucoup* also goes out to everyone at the Ritz Hotel.

❊❊❊

Finally, thank you to Jerrod Allen and Fiona Baker, for making my life rich beyond measure.

ABOUT THE AUTHOR

Karen Karbo is the author of three novels, all of which were named *New York Times* Notable Books. *The Stuff of Life: A Daughter's Memoir* was a People Magazine's Critics' Choice and winner of the Oregon Book Award for Creative Nonfiction. A past winner of the General Electric Foundation Award for Younger Writers, Karen is, in addition, the recipient of a grant from the National Endowment for the Arts. Her essays, articles, and reviews have appeared in the *New York Times, Outside, Elle, Vogue, More,* and *salon.com.* Her most recent work is *How to Hepburn: Lessons on Living from Kate the Great.* She lives in Portland, Oregon, where she is still hunting for a piece of vintage Chanel couture.